Preshal works in Lint  deprived areas in the C many fine families living it having a very active community spirit, it has more than its fair share of problems. Poverty, deprivation, alcohol and drug abuse, family breakdown and youth crime all go to make it a challenging place to work but Preshal thrives on the challenge. Its doors are open five days a week and on Sunday evenings too. Everyone is welcome. Although Preshal seeks to meet the social needs that present themselves it is unashamedly Christian in its approach and none the worse for that. Many who went in the door in the depths of despair have found hope and purpose. A good number have even found faith in God. *More Miracles from Mayhem* tells the stories of some of those who go in and out of Preshal, whether as Board or staff members, volunteers or local folk looking for support. Preshal serves them all and they serve Preshal. That's one of the beauties of Preshal, everyone is hands-on and that's what gets things done.

Sir Tom Farmer

Having met May Nicholson for the first time only a few months ago I have been captivated by the work she does in my home area of Govan.

My meeting with May was arranged by my good friend John McLaughlin who in his own marvellous way does so much for so many charities and young people that when he says he wants me to meet someone special, then it is almost a duty to obey him.

May's story is one of courage, determination and belief in God that not only captivated me, but inspired me in the knowledge that all those Govanites who have experienced similar problems as May are in good hands because her drive and care for them will meet no bounds.

I was born in Govan in 1941 and brought up in one of the toughest areas, the corner of Govan Road and Neptune Street, then known as the Irish Channel, given the number of Irish families who had left their home country, and yes there were gangs then – Burndyke Street, Sharpe Street and Nethan Street. I can recall some gang fights as I can recall some pretty tough characters, but they tended to fight one another. There was a great saying in those days "Liberty Taker" and even the hardest of these gangs could not tolerate "Liberty Takers" and they would soon be sorted out.

Tackling modern problems today is entirely different, as in Govan in bygone days had close family communities. Today we are depending on people like May Nicholson to create organisations to help our youth and get them to listen to sound advice in order to lead them to a better life away from crime and drugs, trusting the very people who have been down that same road, but had the will and determination to do something with their lives and are better for it.

I wish May every success in her building project and I am confident that with all the right help it will be done.

Sir Alex Ferguson C.B.E.,
Manchester United Football Club

More Miracles from Mayhem is a compelling account of the lives of some of those who have been associated with a project in Govan, Glasgow, set up by May Nicholson to provide an open door five days a week and on Sunday evenings for anyone who feels like coming in.

The variety of circumstances of deprivation in which many of those people were, until they met with May or came to the project, is huge but they have a feature in common. When the Lord Jesus by His Spirit came into these lives, His entry made a remarkable difference. His entry produced miracles indeed. The stories are narrated in a very clear direct way which I found compelling.

We live in a very materialistic age but these stories are a powerful testimony to the fact that the life of the Spirit is fundamental to our existence as human beings. I hope that reading about these miracles will prove a powerful incentive to the reader to pray that Jesus will come into his life, to effect a profound change of the same kind as that which many of these who are the subject miracles experienced.

The name of the project is Preshal, which is the Gaelic word for precious. As I said, it is an open door to every one who wishes to enter as May and her colleagues have a marvellous ability to welcome and help those who come and to direct them to Jesus as the One who can welcome and cater for the needs, material and spiritual, of the chief of sinners.

Lord Mackay of Clashfern
Lord Chancellor 1987-1997

More Miracles from Mayhem

The Continuing Story of
May Nicholson and the Preshal Trust

Irene Howat

CHRISTIAN
FOCUS

Copyright © May Nicholson 2009

ISBN 978-1-84550-449-6

Published in 2009,
Reprinted 2010 and 2017
by
Christian Focus Publications,
Geanies House, Fearn,
Ross-shire, IV20 1TW, Scotland

www.christianfocus.com

Cover design by Daniel Van Straaten

Printed and bound by
Norhaven, Denmark

Contents

Dedication:

For all of Preshal's precious people
and in memory of
Lucas Alexander Meacock

Foreword
by Betty Souter

My husband and I didn't know about Preshal until a friend told us about it. She had visited the project and was very taken with the work it was doing. Our friend knows about social work and we valued her opinion highly. Among the things she told us was that Preshal was running on a shoe-string. My husband and I run The Souter Charitable Trust, and we were able to send a gift to help Preshal at that time.

As my background is in social work I was interested to visit Preshal to see what was going on there and I was very impressed. It seems to me that Preshal is a bit like a lighthouse and May is the lighthouse keeper. It's in a poor and dark part of Glasgow and its light shines out and attracts people to it. There are so many people living in dysfunctional families, or who have no families at all, and the community aspect of Preshal is a real blessing to them. It helps to get people out of their isolation, whatever the cause of it.

May and Preshal do what they can and go the second mile too. The sad thing is that the government has more or less withdrawn from funding Christian organisations, even though it is they who still go the second mile, which is what makes a difference in people's lives.

1

Looking at my Friend

I met May Nicholson for the first time at a conference in a remote and beautiful corner of Argyll. At that time May was working with Glasgow City Mission and she had brought some of the ladies who went to the Mission's Family Centre in Govan up to the weekend conference. I was the speaker, and just before I was to give my talk, May came, put her hands on my shoulders, and prayed for God's blessing. God answered that prayer and one of the ladies whom May had brought with her came to saving faith in Jesus.

Although I was the speaker, May did a lot of talking. She's never short of words. By the time we parted I had come to love her, and over the months and years that have passed since then, our love has grown and deepened. May's regular goodbye on the phone is 'I love you millions' and I love her millions too. I've watched with great interest as the Lord led May to start Preshal and as it has grown and been blessed.

A visit to Preshal is precious, and so it should be, as the word Preshal comes from the Gaelic for precious. For one thing, a blanket of love surrounds you as you go in. My first visits were made when I was writing *Miracles from Mayhem*, the story of May's life. If I thought the warm welcome was because I was writing May's book, I was very mistaken. Preshal's welcome is for everyone who comes through the door, and I'm not alone in enjoying the warm blanket of love.

Another thing that surprises people when I take them to Preshal (and I've taken a number of friends to visit) is that you can't tell who are members of staff and who are local men and women in need of the support Preshal offers. Of course, part of that is that the one feeds into the other. Those who come to Preshal needing help sometimes go on to be volunteers and then members of staff. That's one of the beauties of the place. A third thing that I love is the easy way in which conversations move from ordinary day-to-day things to the Lord. There's no embarrassment about speaking of Jesus; there's no awkwardness when two people sitting at a table doing craft work stop and pray together about a problem they've been sharing. Recently I took a friend to visit Preshal. We walked to the door with May and Mary Doll (you'll read her moving story in the book). In the busy entrance hall the four of us stopped and Mary Doll prayed God's blessing on my friend and me as we left. People were coming in and out past us and nobody thought it odd that four of us should be standing there praying.

May came through the rocky road of alcoholism, drug abuse and many of the things that go with them, but God has used her awful experiences to His glory. She has also gone through cancer. Just after she was diagnosed, I picked May up from a hospital appointment. As she got into the car, she turned to me and said, 'Well, God has used me being an alcoholic to let me reach out to alcoholics. Now he'll use me having cancer to help me reach out to people with cancer.'

At the end of *Miracles from Mayhem* May was going through treatment for her cancer. Some years have passed and she's now in good health and praising God for it. But over the time of May's treatment the work at Preshal went on without her. Another thing I love about it is that Preshal, while it was started by May, is not her baby. She's not jealous of what other people do;

rather she helps people grow their gifts in order that she can do other things. It's only because her team of workers are given freedom to use and develop their skills in Preshal that she can travel all over the place talking about the work. And when she does that, she often takes people with her who came to Preshal with burdens wearing them down, and who now can give testimony to God's ability to save from the deepest of dark pits.

Miracles from Mayhem was May's story. This is not. *More Miracles from Mayhem* is about people who have come through Preshal's door, either needing help or as helpers. As in Preshal, so in the book; it's hard to tell which is which, for those who come to help are helped, and those who come needing support end up supporting other people.

2

A Mother and Daughter look back

I don't remember too much about family life, but I do remember the day it ended. It started as an ordinary school day, but some people arrived at our school in Glasgow and took my two brothers, two sisters and me from our classrooms, and the next thing we knew we were in a children's home in Dunoon. It wasn't all that many miles away but it might as well have been on the moon. Glasgow was the only home we'd ever known. My sisters and I spent almost a year in Dunoon but our two young brothers were fostered up in the north of Scotland for part of the time. Nobody explained why we were in a home. I don't suppose anyone realised how confused and upset we were. We thought it might be because Dad was in the Army, and maybe that was right enough.

One day, just out of the blue, Dad arrived in Dunoon with a strange woman at his side. 'We're going to get married,' he told us. 'This is your new mum.' Our new mum was a widow with two children of her own. We'd only begun to get used to the idea when we were taken from Dunoon back to Glasgow. My older sister and one of my brothers went to stay with our gran. My younger sister and brother and I went with Dad. Our stepmother was good enough to us, but she had two children of her own and we knew they always came first. That wasn't anything new as we'd never been first in the queue for anything in the children's home. Dad and our stepmother had a son, but by then I was growing up and beginning to think about moving away. When I left school, a friend and I decided that we'd go down to England to work. Many a night was spent planning our lives, and the day eventually came when we waved goodbye to Glasgow and set off for the south. For the next four years we worked in hotels and hospitals, both places that provided us with somewhere to stay.

My friend went back to Glasgow before I did, but I wasn't long behind her. It was all change at home, for my stepmother had gone to live with her father and the house I'd lived in had been given to cousins. So I went to my gran and it was there that I met Alex, the man I was to marry when I was twenty-one. He was a fine figure of a man, an electric welder and a hard worker. There was no slacking in those days. You learned to graft when you were young and, if you didn't, your boss soon found someone to replace you. Like most of the men around us, my man worked hard during the week and drank hard at weekends.

Over the years we had six children, but lost one of them as a baby. Maybe it was because there were nappies everywhere, and children everywhere too, that Alex spent more and more time at the pub. Of course, the more he spent on drink, the less money there was coming in for the children. Times were hard, but they were no harder for me than they were for many young mothers just like me. We didn't talk much about our problems though; a kind of pride kept us from admitting to each other what we all knew. When I really started worrying was when I realised that Alex was drinking at work as well as in the pub. 'You're going to end up getting the sack,' I told him. Before he did, and left us with nothing to pay the bills, I started taking wee jobs to earn what I could. I found a good job as a train cleaner. It was hard graft. Most of the time I worked nights and during the day I was there for the children when they needed me.

Sometimes I felt like running away, but I had nowhere to run to. In fact, I did pack up and take the children away once or twice when Alex was drinking hard. We went to my sister then, but I always went back. My man needed me. There were no refuges for women and children then; we just had to make the best of it. Mothers used to tell their daughters when they got married that they'd made their bed and would have to lie in it.

Welders need to be sober so it was only a matter of time before Alex lost his job because the drink had got the better of him and he couldn't stop. Once, when it had made him really ill, the doctor put him in hospital and warned him that he'd need to stop for the sake of his health. To be fair, he did stop for a time, and he was a different person when he wasn't drinking. Our home was a different place when he was sober. The whole family was different when there was no booze in the house. It was great while it lasted, but it didn't last long. And when he started drinking again, he stopped eating, and that worried me. It wasn't like Alex to let me send for the doctor, but one day he knew he was ill and needed help. The doctor came and said he had a very bad chest infection. But he never made it to the hospital. He died that afternoon lying on the couch in the living room. The strangest thing happened that day. 'Betty,' I said to my daughter as Alex died, 'there's someone standing on each side of me.' I wasn't a Christian then and didn't recognise that God's angels were looking after me. But I know that now.

I kept on working on the railway until I retired, though my job changed. After a long time cleaning trains I was promoted to checking the trains after the cleaners had finished. Although I wasn't strong, I managed to keep going. After I retired I looked for a wee job to keep me going and got one cleaning premises belonging to Glasgow City Mission. May Nicholson worked there as a city missionary and that's where I got to know her. From the day we met I knew I had a special friend in May. And the thing is, that's how hundreds of people feel and every one of them really is special to her, because she knows that everyone's special to God.

Once, May asked me to go with her to church. That very first night I gave my heart to the Lord and became a Christian. That's more than six years ago and it was the very, very best thing I ever did. From then on I often went to meetings when May was speaking. Not only that, but sometimes I've even spoken myself about what the Lord has done for me. Imagine that! Me, wee Nancy, speaking at a meeting! The first time I could hardly speak for crying, but other folk there were crying too when they heard my story. I love talking about Jesus because he's so wonderful to me. I don't mean that life's easy; it's not. I'm getting older and I'm not really very fit. But God has given me peace and calm and a good family too.

Back to my family. One of my brothers died when he was just twenty-one. He took his own life. My other brother married, had two children, and then went out to Australia. He and his family are all Christians now. My brother's daughter is already in heaven as she was killed in a car crash. My half-brother is a Christian too, an elder in a church in Glasgow. It's wonderful to be part of a Christian family, and who would ever have believed it when you think back to how our lives started?

I was a cleaner when I met May, but she promoted me to tea and toast maker when she left Glasgow City Mission and started Preshal in St Kenneth's Church Hall in Govan. And you'll never guess what – I'm now a member of the Preshal Board! When May told me the Board wanted me to join, I didn't believe her. Then she said that the Duchess of Montrose thought I would be good on the Board. The Duchess is President of Preshal. I don't know what I have to say, but I'm just myself and, I suppose, I understand the Govan people's backgrounds. Most of the Board members don't know what it's like not to have any money at all and have children to feed, but I understand that because I've been there. It's sad though. When I was young we all thought it would get better for families one day. But there are mothers coming to Preshal today who are as poor as I was all those years ago.

If anyone had ever told me that I would meet a duchess, I'd have laughed at them, yet now I can call Cathy Montrose my friend. One of my wee jobs when the children were young was working in a butcher's factory. My bit of the production line linked sausages. Once, not long ago, I met the man who owned that factory at a garden party which the Duchess of Montrose was giving. When I told him I used to link sausages in his factory, he must have smiled at me getting from there to being at a duchess's garden party!

'Preshal means 'precious' and I feel treasured. The first time I felt that was when Alex died and God's angels were with me. But over the years, especially since I became a Christian, I've had so many times of feeling treasured. Simple things happen that show me how much God cares about me. One day I came out of a shop laden with bags. The family are always telling me that they'll do my shopping, but I don't like bothering them. That day a wee boy of eight or nine stopped right in front of me and looked at me. 'Listen, son,' I said, 'could you help me across the road? I stay just over there.' The wee boy took nearly all the bags and he even carried them up the stair for me. 'Thanks very much,' I said, and I opened my bag to give him some money.

'I don't want anything,' he replied.

'You can buy some juice and crisps,' I told him.

'No,' he said. 'I'm just going to my gran.'

'Where does your gran stay?' I asked.

She stayed up the very next close! God had stopped just exactly the right wee boy in front of me! Some people would say it was silly seeing God in things like that. But I know that's His way of showing me how precious I am to Him. And He's shown me how precious I am by giving me a great family too.

I've got dreams for Preshal and I think about them when I pass the local chemist and see a whole queue of folk waiting for their methadone. There are so many needy people in Govan, and my dream is that Preshal will be able to reach out to them and that they'll discover that they are precious too. Maybe one day there will be a queue waiting outside Preshal all wanting to hear about Jesus.

Sandra's Story

I've known May for about seven years and she means the world to me. I'm Nancy's daughter and I've seen all that May has done for Mum over the years. They are really good friends. Mum often stays at May's house at weekends, and when May had cancer Mum helped look after her. That's what life's about, being helped and helping other people.

My husband was murdered when our girls were 13 and 11. The years after that were bad and Mum did all she could to help us through. She was great. Now I have two grandchildren. I became a Christian two years ago and God has helped me through quite a hard time. I have a son called Jay, and he was diagnosed with severe autism when he was about eighteen months old. He's four now and his dad Ricky and I love him to bits and wouldn't change him for the world.

Although Jay can only say a few words, usually he doesn't speak at all. He likes to be on his own and doesn't really like other people apart from Ricky and me and his granny. He's lovely with the three of us. He doesn't even like coming to Preshal because he hates crowds of people. We're limited where we can go with Jay and he's best just in our own house and our own garden. Thankfully we have a big garden with a slide in it. He likes that.

Jay is at nursery now and a special bus comes to take him there. I used to worry that he'd never go away from me, but when the nursery bus stops at the house he doesn't even look back to wave to me! He'll go to school in the same place as his nursery. That means that he won't have a change as that could upset him. Autism isn't an illness; it's a condition and we just have to get used to Jay having it. As long as

I keep his routine the same every day, things go fine. In many ways Jay is a very clever boy. He loves reading and he can read from the computer screen, even words like 'insect' and he's not at school yet! He can also write things on the computer without even looking at the keys. He likes sequences and he can press the numbers one to fifty on my telephone keypad. That kind of thing isn't hard for him.

At first when Jay was diagnosed I was worried about his future. But God has given me peace about that. He made Jay the way he is and He knows what's best for his life. Ricky is great with him and we do our best for Jay together. Mum is a really good granny to him too, though she finds him a bit of a handful sometimes. Although I can't bring Jay to Preshal because he's frightened of people, I come myself when I can. In the tough times when my girls were younger, Preshal gave me a reason to look forward to every day. Now, if I'm down, coming to Preshal picks me up again. Everyone has problems and coming to Preshal reminds me that I'm not the only one with problems. That's the thing about troubles. When you have them you think you're alone. Preshal reminds me that I'm no different from anyone else, apart from knowing that Jesus is my Saviour and He'll see me through.

3

Looking at the Beginning

When I was a girl growing up in Ferguslie Park in Paisley in the 1950s there wasn't any need for a place like Preshal because, although everyone was poor, we lived in a real community. In the last fifty years we've lost the 'unity' out of 'community'. If there was a problem, the women sat and talked about it, sharing their cares and their worries. Sometimes they just sat on their doorsteps, still wearing their peenies (aprons), and talked and talked.

Maybe the women in Ferguslie Park looked as if they were wasting their time. They weren't.

Apart from anything else, they needed to sit down for the rest. Bringing up a family is hard work, but it was even harder then. Women did the washing bent over scrubbing boards, rubbing the clothes up and down the hard ridges until their shoulders ached and their hands were sore, thanks to the hard soap they used. Bigger washings were trampled in the bath, if they had a bath, and then wrung through the mangle before being hung out in dry weather or hung all over the living room if it was wet. Vacuum cleaners were unheard of and even carpet sweepers weren't all that common because most of us had linoleum on the floors. On floor washing day the wet linoleum was covered with sheets of newspaper and children were chased outside until the paper seeped up the damp and the floor was dry. And you could forget clean underwear every day. Our underwear lasted a week, and school shirts got their collars and cuffs rubbed with a soapy cloth to make them last all week as well.

Things children take for granted now just didn't happen then. Mothers cut everyone's hair, and if one of the neighbours was good at it, she did all the local hairdressing. Hair-washing was a weekly event, usually done on Fridays, and normally followed by the dreaded nit-comb. We sat down on a hard chair with a newspaper underneath it and our hair was tugged through a fine metal comb to get rid of any lice and nits. We weren't dirty; even the poshest Glasgow children would have had their hair nit-combed weekly fifty years ago. And we didn't use shampoo either. It was ordinary soap for our hair and Mum used soap powder for the dishes. I was nearly grown up before washing-up liquid was common.

Clothes were patched and darned until the patches and darns joined together, and what could be passed on from one child to another was passed on and on and on. Things were passed down in families and between neighbours too. Of course there were fall-outs, but neighbours were real neighbours. That was a case of 'have to do.' You had to get on with each other because everybody needed everyone else, in good times and in bad. Fall-outs were short, sharp and mostly soon forgotten, through there were some families who just didn't get on with each other from generation to generation.

When there was a death in Ferguslie Park everybody knew what to do. Somebody would help wash and lay out the body; someone else would take away the children and look after them. A sheet would be taken round the doors and a collection arranged for the bereaved family. Other neighbours made the sandwiches and scones that were needed for visitors in the mourning house. Biscuits weren't really a big thing then. Folk who hardly had two pennies to rub together gave what they had, and sometimes did without things themselves, to help a neighbour in trouble.

People shared what they had in good times, even if the good times came illegally through a local employer. All our paintwork was the same colour, thanks to the men who worked in the shipyards – the very same colour that was used on ships. I don't suppose any of the shipyard bosses ever walked down our street and recognised where the paint had come from! Our curtains were all the same material too. Strange that!

And neighbours looked out for each other's children too. If Mrs Brown skelped me on the backside for doing something, and Mum heard about it, Mum would skelp me for being skelped! She would never have thought of checking up why Mrs Brown had punished me. If a neighbour punished you, you'd done something to deserve it. And if you'd done something to deserve it, then you deserved it again when you got home. Changed days! Nobody in Ferguslie Park knew they had any 'rights', certainly not the children.

We were poor; we were all poor. In fact, our part of Paisley was one of the poorest places in Europe when I was growing up. But we didn't know we were poor and we were no worse than anyone else in the street, and better off than some. So there was no need for a place like Preshal. People knew each other, they understood each other and they helped each other when they could. Children and young folk were known by name, and you can get up to a lot less mischief when everybody knows you and knows your mother.

When I was fifteen years old I had choices to make. I could have chosen the right or the wrong, and I chose the wrong. I didn't do that because anyone made me, but because I wanted to. I chose of my own free will to go down the wrong road. When a girl I knew asked if I wanted to chip in for a half bottle of wine, I happily handed over the money. Then I went up a close (an alley) and took my first mouthful of the stuff and discovered confidence for the first time. Cheek I'd had before, plenty of it, but never confidence, and that felt really good. I'd always felt a misfit, even in my family. I was certainly always a misfit in school and I was out of it as soon as I could be. There were times when I imagined I'd been adopted because I felt so out of place at home, everywhere.

I was still fifteen when I was taken to hospital in a drunken and drugged coma and I was there for months. In a way hospital suited me. I didn't need to think. We had no choices to make. Clothes appeared and we put them on. Food arrived on the table and we ate it. We sat most of the day stoned out of our minds with the drugs we were given. I went from being stoned with drink and illegal drugs to be stoned with what was brought to me by nurses. And being stoned suited me; it stopped me feeling. When I eventually got out of hospital the first thing I thought of was getting another drink. Drink took away my self respect and even my sanity – I mean that – and it could easily have taken my life. There are people I used to drink with who didn't survive their addiction.

My wee mother used to break her heart. 'Is it me? Is it me?' she asked, over and over and over again. We'd been poor right enough, but she'd brought up my older brothers and sisters without them going off the rails and breaking her heart. I cried too and asked, 'Why am I like this?' There was no answer for Mum. And the only answer for me was that I was a drunk and a junkie because that's what I'd chosen to be. Dad, who was dead by then, was a Friday drinker, like most of the men in the area. So I knew what drinking was about and the problems it could cause in a home, yet I still chose to go down that road myself. Eventually my family met and made a decision: they'd get rid of the problem, and the problem might get better if it was out of the road. At first the idea was to send me to America, but I persuaded them to let me go to Jersey instead. I had a cousin there and I thought that he and I could live it up together. So with Mum's money in my pocket I set out for my new life.

There's a story in the Bible that was my story. Jesus spoke about a prodigal son who persuaded his father to give him his share of the family money and he went off and spent it all. As long as he had money he had plenty of friends, but when his money ran out they were nowhere to be seen. He had to go down to the pits – looking after a herd of pigs and eating pigswill because he was so hungry – before he came to his senses. And when he did, he went right home to his father, who threw a party because his son had come back. I was like that prodigal. I took my mum's money, and she must have scrimped and saved to give it to me, and headed off for the bright lights of Jersey.

My cousin and I had a great time ... until we heard about ourselves on the radio news. The police were looking for a couple from Glasgow who had stolen and crashed a car. I wasn't sober enough to remember how I got there, but the next thing I knew I was in Blackpool, penniless and on the streets. I didn't know the story of the prodigal son then, but I sure knew what he felt like. After a couple of nights sleeping on the streets I made a reversed charge call to Mum's neighbour and asked Mum to wire money to a post office in Blackpool to get me home. Although she hated what I was doing to myself, Mum loved me. She wired enough for my bus fare and, when I arrived home, there was a big pan of stovies on the cooker and the water was heated for a bath. Years later my cousin became a Christian, but that's a different story.

God loves sinners although he hates their sin. He loves sinners so much that He gave his Son Jesus to die on the cross so that our sin could be taken away from us forever. Now, I have a daughter and a son, and there's not one person in this universe that I'd consider giving their lives for. Yet our Father God loved sinners, even drink-crazed sinners, so much, that's what He did. God is so holy that He can't even look on sin. So there's no way any single one of us could go to heaven to be with Him, for we are all miserable sinners whether we know it or not, whether we are drunks and drug addicts or 'respectable'. Sin needs to be punished, and the amazing thing is that Jesus, God's Son, willingly accepted our punishment on the cross so that those who believe in Him should be washed clean and taken home to heaven when they die. My brain can't begin to take that in, but God's Word says it, so it's true. God doesn't tell lies.

To cut a long story short (you can read the longer version in *Miracles from Mayhem*), I married and had a daughter, Tracey. You would have thought that having a lovely wee daughter would have stopped me drinking; it didn't. Mum and the rest of my family came to Tracey's rescue many a time when I was drunk and incapable. They took her and looked after her until I sobered up before bringing her back to me. I promised that wee girl the whole world, yet I didn't stop drinking. She wasn't neglected, Mum saw to that, but she was neglected of her mother's love. It hurts me to say that, but it's true. You can't starve a child of her mother's love without there being consequences. But I thank God that, all these years later, Tracey is my best friend. Not only that, but she works in Preshal, and she knows from her own experience how much it is needed. So many of the people who come to Preshal have backgrounds like Tracey's, but they don't always have grannies and aunties to love them through the hard times. She didn't learn it from me, but Tracey is a wonderful mum and I thank God for that.

When Tracey was ten her wee brother was born. Although I'd spent a lot of my pregnancy in a psychiatric hospital, God gave us a lovely healthy baby boy. I can still remember my disgust at myself, and my horror at the thought of my life contaminating this beautiful baby. Before we left the maternity unit I promised Alan that he'd have a very different start to life from his big sister. He didn't. He was a toddler when I sobered up enough one morning to realise that Alan was wandering around the house in yesterday's clothes and still wearing yesterday's nappy. That hit me like a ton of bricks. Apart from my family, there was only one other person who would ever let me into her house, and I changed and dressed Alan and then went to see her.

It turned out that she was going to a meeting that night and I said I'd go with her, though I'd no idea where she was going. It could have been a bingo club for all I knew. She tried to put me off, telling me I was filthy (true), disgusting (true), and that my clothes were a mess (all of this was true) and that I wasn't going with her. If she'd asked me to go, I'd probably have backed out of it, but her attitude made me determined. I followed her and landed at a Staurus meeting, a collection of former alcoholics who were trying to keep off the drink with God's help.

When I followed my friend in I found a group of people sitting in a circle singing! I was so embarrassed – for them, not for me. Then they read a bit from a book I didn't understand and I didn't know was the Bible. After that there was a prayer, and by the time one of the men prayed for me I was in floods of tears. I didn't think I was worth a prayer. All these years later (that was in 1981 and I was thirty-four years old) I still remember the words of his prayer; they burnt into my heart. He prayed, 'Lord, I pray for that wee woman you've brought here tonight. We can all see that she's filthy by looking at the outside of her, but you know how much more filthy her heart is. Touch her and clean her.' God answered that prayer and I left the meeting a forgiven sinner.

4

Looking out

May's Story – 2

As soon as I was a Christian I had a great love for people who didn't know Jesus and I was worried that they were going to hell. Maybe I did it all wrong, but I was a missionary from day one. I used to go round the streets, knocking at doors and telling whoever would listen that Jesus was my Saviour and he was willing to be their Saviour too. Some of them must have thought that the drink had finally blown my mind. But there were others who could see the difference in my life, and was there a difference! My house was clean, my children had a mother, and I was sober day and night. I could never have done any of that myself. God did it all, every single bit of it.

One of the first things I did was phone my psychiatrist and tell him that I'd found the answer to his patients' problems. He must have thought I was out of my mind! One of my first ministries was to go back to my psychiatric hospital to talk to the patients. Because we had spent so much time together I knew when some of their birthdays were and I used to take cakes in to celebrate with them. A couple in my church had been reading the Bible and God had spoken to them about how they could hold out helping hands. He led them to open a half-way house for patients being discharged from that hospital and their work continues to this day, though now on a smaller scale.

If I'd known God's plans, I would never have believed they were possible. But God is great. The Bible says, "'For I know the plans I have for you,'" declares the Lord, "plans to prosper you and not to harm you, plans to give you a hope and a future. Then you will call upon me and come and pray to me, and I will listen to you. You will seek me and find me when you seek me with all your heart'" (Jeremiah 29:11-13).

This is how His plans have worked out over the years. Soon after I became a Christian I went to St Ninian's Church in Ferguslie Park, and I felt like a hand going into a glove. For someone who had never fitted in anywhere (at least, not when I was sober) I was totally blown away by the feeling of being part of the Christian church. It was my family. Amazingly, I became part of the ministry team, reaching out to the people in the area, especially those with addiction problems. Then God's plan took an unexpected twist when I was asked to go as a Church of Scotland project worker to a deprived area of Dundee! Me?

My minister went through to Dundee with me to see the project and to try to discover if this was what God wanted me to do. Before we went, I said to him, 'If the man we are going to see quotes the verse from the Bible that says, "The Spirit of the Sovereign Lord is on me, because the Lord has anointed me to preach good news to the poor" (Isaiah 61:1), I'll know that I'm meant to go.' It's hard to describe how hard it was even to think about leaving the church in Ferguslie Park. I'd felt an outsider all of my life, and for the first time I really felt part of something; I felt I belonged. To be honest, I was heartbroken at the very thought of going to Dundee. That day, after showing my minister and me round the project, our host walked with us to the car. 'Do you know what brought me to work here?' he asked, before we parted. And then he quoted the exact words of the verse God had laid on my heart for guidance. 'The Spirit of the Sovereign Lord is on me, because the Lord has anointed me to preach good news to the poor.' I didn't want to leave Ferguslie Park, but God had spoken and I had absolutely no choice. Alan and I moved through to Dundee. Tracey stayed in Paisley because she was just about to be married. Only a mother can know what it felt like to leave her behind.

After three years of hard work in Dundee, I was invited to become a Glasgow City Missionary. You know the expression, 'you could have knocked me over with a feather'? Well, you could have done. God showed me that was what He wanted me to do and Alan and I moved back to Glasgow to work in a Glasgow City Mission Child and Family Centre in Govan. And that's where I met Nancy, whose story is told at the beginning of the book. God wanted me in Govan, I knew that right from the start, but He took me there to begin a different work.

Nine years later the time was right to leave Glasgow City Mission and start an outreach work which eventually became Preshal. It was June 2002. The name Preshal means precious, and our aim is to tell people, who often feel as much of a misfit as I once did, that they are precious to God who made them, and that they are precious to us too. Our first meeting place was St Kenneth's Church hall. The minister, Rev. David Keddie, was a great support and a real encourager. Since then we have moved to other premises, and, as this book is being written, our vision is to have our own purpose-built building. We don't want a castle; we just want a home that fits what we do.

What do we do? The best way to describe what happens inside (and outside) Preshal is to go through the week. On Sunday evenings we have a fellowship meeting and we get a good number coming to that. The talks are simple, but some of them stay in my mind for ages. One man brought some sweets along. He had Refreshers, Smarties, Liquorice Allsorts and Good News chocolates. He asked what kind of people we were. Were we Smarties, always one up on everyone else? Were we Refreshers, the kind of people who did other folk good? Then he said that it didn't matter what kind of people we were, God loved Allsorts: all kinds, all ages, all colours, all abilities, all social classes. And then he went on to say that we could be like Good News chocolates, if we believed in the Lord Jesus Christ, because then we would pass on the good news about Him to the people we met.

God had been prompting me for a time to arrange for people who have been converted to be discipled, to be taught the Word. We've not only got to be born again, but we've to grow as Christians too. Recently we started a discipleship class. Manu, a lovely Christian friend from India – you'll read about him later – takes the class for an hour before the fellowship meeting.

Every morning there is a mixture of arts and crafts. You'd be amazed at the cards, découpage, paintings and jewellery that are made! There's also pool, a selection of card games and things like that. Counselling goes on all the time as it's needed and we are there to help people with things such as filling in forms. On Monday mornings there is also an information technology class. On Monday afternoons we have our art class as well as one-to-one literacy and numeracy teaching.

Tuesdays are spent on games plus our usual activities. That's followed by our lunch club and an afternoon of quizzes. We now have a youth work on Tuesday evenings, reaching out to some of the most troubled young people in the area. When we started our youth work someone suggested that we go round the schools advertising it. But I didn't feel that was the right thing to do at all. The kind of kids we want to reach aren't in school; they're excluded, expelled or just not attending. We want to reach the kids who are gathering in gangs in Elder Park, who are involved in gang fighting and knife crime there. The youth work is relatively new, but things are moving forward all the time.

On Wednesday mornings it's keep-fit time with line dancing. Alan often takes the men fishing on Wednesday mornings. They go down the coast and fish off one of the piers before heading for an ice cream in the summer or a cup of tea if it's cold. Art, literacy and numeracy take up the afternoons. Thursday morning is much the same as Monday and then we have a lunch club. There are games in the afternoon. Friday is cookery morning followed by digital photography in the afternoon.

Whatever activities are taking place, there is always plenty going on in the background. People don't sit on their doorsteps and talk about their problems in Glasgow now, but many of them sit in Preshal and chat. Problems are shared and often solutions are found. And it's not at all unusual to find groups of two and three talking about the Lord Jesus. Jesus said that where two or three are gathered together in His name, He is there in the midst of them. I'm very conscious of His presence in Preshal and we see the results in souls saved and lives changed.

We have a caravan at Saltcoats where many of our people have gone for short breaks. When you are hard up, the thought of a holiday seems impossible and it's like a dream come true to get away to the seaside for a few days. In 2007, ninety-two families spent time at the caravan. Of course, some people couldn't get away even if they wanted to, and Preshal tries to reach out to them too. A group goes to Shotts Prison every week and an average of twenty-two prisoners meet with us. A new work has now begun in HMP Cornton Vale in Stirling.

In all of the Christian work I've been involved in, my aim is to do myself out of a job. I did that in Ferguslie Park, in Dundee, and I believe I also did it in the work I was doing for Glasgow City Mission. I hope and pray that I'm doing that right now in Preshal, and for a time that looked necessary. When *Miracles from Mayhem* was published I was being treated for breast cancer. Some lovely people who read the book even phoned Preshal to see how I was keeping!

Preshal isn't a one man band. Now there's a team of workers: six full-time (including Alan and Tracey), six part-time and four sessional workers. The team was much smaller when I had cancer, but they pulled together and the work went on. I hope I'll live to see my grandchildren growing up, but if God were to take me home to heaven today, I believe that the work of Preshal is established and it would continue without me. Of course, there would be changes, but I'd not be there to argue with them!

Being diagnosed with cancer is scary. The first thing that came into my mind was that I had to get my affairs in order and I did that as best I could. Tracey and Alan were upset when I told them and we prayed together about it. I told God that I'd really like time with my grandchildren. I'd love them to remember me as a granny who played with them and prayed with them, a granny they had pillow fights with and who told them stories about Jesus. I wasn't afraid of death, but I didn't like the thought of dying. I know where I'm going when I die and I'm looking forward to heaven when my time comes.

Before I had my operation a few friends came to the house and prayed with me. I felt the touch of God that night. The next day, after I was admitted, a group of women arrived to visit me. They were from Seagate Evangelical Church in Troon and I'd met them when I'd gone there to speak. Between six and eight women arrived and prayed for about an hour with me, especially about my fear of the anaesthetic. I felt the better for their visit, and even when they went away I wasn't left alone, for I was very conscious of God with me.

The operation went well and it was followed by chemotherapy. That was hard going. There were days when I felt all right and others when I didn't have what it took to do anything at all. I went to Preshal whenever I was able, but because of the risk of infection I had to be careful. Infections were a real problem, so much so that I wasn't able to have my last chemotherapy treatment because

I was so ill. There were times when I was very, very poorly. When I lost my hair I bought three wigs: one blond, one red and one brown. When I felt glamorous (you only feel glamorous occasionally on chemo!) I wore the blond one. When I felt dangerous (!) I wore the red one, and the brown one was for everyday use. Those who came about the house knew that there were times when I just wore a turban to keep my head warm because I didn't even feel up to my everyday self.

Alan was always getting colds, so he often couldn't come near me. But he was always there to do things that needed to be done, and there was plenty for him to do. He was a real source of strength to me. Tracey cleaned and cooked and looked after her mum. It's not always easy for a mum to be looked after by her daughter, but Tracey was brilliant. I used to worry that she was wearing herself out. God knew that, and sometimes He sent help from surprising places. One day I had a phone call from a young man in Ireland. Preshal and a group in Ireland called Wellspring have a lot in common and we keep closely in touch. This young man said that the Lord had laid it on his heart to come and minister to me for a weekend. As I knew that would give Tracey a break, I was happy to accept his offer. The young man came and cooked and cleaned and looked after me. He was a gift from God.

Another night I was lying in bed caput. I didn't have the energy to pray as I felt absolute rubbish. I couldn't even sit up. So I lay there and meditated on the Lord, thinking especially about the Bible story of the woman who had been ill for twelve years. She believed that if she could only touch the hem of Jesus' cloak, she would be healed. The poor woman came up behind the Lord in the crowd, reached out, touched the hem of His cloak, and was healed. It's a lovely story. That night, I lay in my bed picturing myself touching the hem of Jesus' cloak. And when I pictured myself doing that, I felt an inner touch from the Lord. I didn't have any more strength. I couldn't have got up out of my bed. But I was given inner strength and deep peace.

Just before the end of my chemotherapy I was really, really ill and in hospital. I was lying in bed aware of a beautiful scene in front of me. There were lovely trees with a path going through them into somewhere I knew was wonderful. I was ready and longing to go along the path when the trees seemed to shut up in front of me and I couldn't go forward. When I was a bit better I realised how near death I had been but that my time hadn't come. There were occasions during my treatment when I felt scared of dying, but that beautiful experience took away my fear of death. Since then I've been able to share that experience with a number of Christians who have told me that they are scared to die.

Radiotherapy was a cakewalk compared to chemotherapy and I felt so much better. The doctors told me that I should try to live life as much like normal as I could. That's what I did, especially after the chemo was over and infections weren't so much of a problem. As I grew stronger and was eventually full time at work again, it was just great to be back at Preshal. But it was greater still to see how it had run over the months of my coming and going. It was a real confirmation to me that the work was the Lord's, not mine. My treatment was successful and it looks as if the cancer isn't coming back, praise the Lord!

It's no fun having cancer, but even at the time I could see good coming out of it. God opened the way for me to have some amazing talks with nurses, doctors and patients, especially young women facing breast cancer. It nearly broke my heart to see some of them because they were in despair and scared stiff. There is still the idea that cancer is a death sentence whatever the statistics say. Nobody ever turned me down when I offered to pray for them and that was a real privilege. Just the other week, years after my treatment, someone who had just been diagnosed with breast cancer came to talk to me about it because she knew I would understand.

Of course, cancer doesn't end with the treatment; there are all the check-ups as well. By the time I was coming to the end of them, I just didn't want to know. I'd had enough. I was enjoying feeling well and I didn't want that peace disturbed by knowing the cancer was still inside me. I had a check-up due and I was seriously thinking of not going. Just then I was due to speak at a meeting in Helensburgh. I was crossing the road to the church when a taxi reversed into me, tossing me in the air and fracturing my pelvis. Instead of speaking at the meeting, I was rushed off by ambulance to hospital. It was late by the time I was taken to the ward and it wasn't long until I drifted off in a doped sleep. The next morning, when I woke up, I saw the woman in the bed next to me reading *Miracles from Mayhem*!

'Are you enjoying that wee book?' I asked her.

'It's great!' she replied. 'Have you read it?'

'Well, you could say I have,' I said, laughing to myself – though laughing out loud was a painful process, thanks to the fractured pelvis!

That afternoon a visitor arrived to see my next-bed-neighbour and she recognised me.

'I was at the rally last week and I bought the book there,' she said. I had been speaking at the Church of Scotland Guild's Annual Meeting the previous week and my book was for sale there!

What a ward that was! I had them all singing choruses, even folk from other wards came to join in. The Ward Sister said she'd never, ever seen a happier ward. Some of the women were facing surgery and were as scared as I had been before my 'op'. I prayed with them before they went to theatre, and one or two of the women told me cares and worries and asked me to pray about them. On the Saturday night I said to them, 'I used to love fish-supper parties. Didn't you?' They all grinned and agreed. 'Well,' said I, 'let's have one. But we'll have to pretend we've got the fish suppers, though we can have the party right enough.' What a great sing-song we had that night.

When you're taken into hospital you have needles stuck in you whether you like it or not. I'd been avoiding going to have my bloods taken for my cancer check-up, and here they were taking them anyway! Afterwards I went to see my GP and everything was fine. And when I went for my mammogram, it was fine too. The thing is, after you've had cancer you can be tempted to expect the worst. I was meant to have that check-up. I didn't go to it; it came to me! I learned a deep lesson over that. While I was being treated for cancer I believe that God showed me that I was going to get better. But when that check-up was due I didn't want to go 'just in case.' A friend reminded me that I had to remember in the darkness what I'd learned in the light. He told me afterwards that he'd used that incident in my life as an illustration in a talk and it really spoke to people as it didn't seem to occur to them that folk like me have spiritual wobbles. If only they knew.

When I went for my last mammogram the radiographer told me that, if this one was clear, it was my final one. It seemed to take ages for the result to come through. And the longer I waited, the more I thought something might be wrong – although I was telling everyone that no news was good news. I used to check the phone answering machine, hoping that there wouldn't be a message from the hospital giving me an appointment. As I was due to go away for a few days, I eventually phoned to get the result. 'It's fine,' the secretary told me. Then she laughed. 'It'll need to be a bus that gets you!'

'Don't say that!' I laughed. 'I was hit by a taxi last year!'

It seems as if the Lord has spared me to Preshal for a while yet, and I'm grateful for that. But it is His work, not mine. And when my time comes I'll hand it over to someone else and thank God for making Jeremiah 29:11 true in my life. '"For I know the plans I have for you," declares the Lord, "plans to prosper you and not to harm you, plans to give you hope and a future."' God's plans have taken me along some very strange roads, but I've gone along them in His company and in the company of His precious people.

5

Looking at Life as Losers

Mary's Story

I was brought up in Glasgow by my dad and mum. I came from a good home and I can't blame my parents for how I've lived my life. They were good examples to me and I'm now trying to be a good example to my daughter. But that's the beginning and the end of the story and it doesn't make much sense without the middle.

Although I had a good home, I was wild right from when I was a girl. I was always in trouble and it must have broken my parents' hearts when the police came to the door looking for me. School finished at three in the afternoon and I'd sometimes not go home until three the next morning. I don't even want to try to imagine what I put my parents through. Dad was very patient with me, but I gave Mum a hard time.

When I was twenty-one I started drinking just to be like my friends. What I didn't know was that they could take their drink and I couldn't. I drank every day and within a year, I would say, I was an alcoholic. It was only when I found myself waking up with the shakes after a night's drinking that I realised I had a problem. The only thing was that my way of coping with a problem was to drink it into oblivion. It was a vicious circle and I was right there in the middle of it.

I don't want to tell my whole story because it involves other people, but it's enough to say that I drank so much that I sometimes didn't know who I was or where I was. Thankfully, the police knew me. Sadly, I've had so much alcohol through my system that my memory is affected. But I suppose there's even a good side to that as there are things I don't want to remember.

During my drinking days I had a son and he's grown up now. He left home and I didn't know where he was. Eventually the police found him and I went to see him. He's a drinker and I explained to him what had happened to me. 'Drink's fun,' he told me, and my heart sank. I remember the days when drink was fun for me, but it wasn't fun for long. I still keep an eye on my boy. He's eighteen now.

It was years later when I had Stephanie and it breaks my heart if I let myself think what I put her through because of drink. Eventually the Social Work Department stepped in and took Stephanie from me. She went to stay with my cousin, who has been great to her. I said that I came from a good family; they are so good that they have stuck by me even when I messed up my life big-style.

I came to Preshal and that was the beginning of a change in my life. At first I wasn't too sure about Christianity. But I listened to what May was saying, and to what other people were saying about the Lord. What was really helpful was that some of the people I spoke to, including May, had been drinkers and they knew God could save even them, because He had. Then suddenly it all made sense. I became a Christian and my world changed!

That was seven months ago and I've not drunk since. I've been sober before for a while and then gone back to drink, but this time it's different. Last time I did it in my own strength, and then ran out of strength to fight drink. This time I'm doing it in God's strength and with the support of Preshal and my great family. He won't let me down and they won't let me down either.

The Social Work Department has given me so many chances in the past I could have understood if they'd given up on me. But they haven't. They've been great, and I really mean that. It's not their fault that I messed up my life and messed up Stephanie's life too. People shouldn't blame social workers for splitting up families; they do everything possible to keep families together, and they are helping me now. I was allocated a house near my family, and near where Stephanie was staying, so she was able to move back in with me and keep the same friends and go to the same school. I've explained to Stephanie that it wasn't her fault that I drank and it wasn't her fault that I couldn't look after her. I've told her that it was her old mummy who was a drunk but her new mummy is different. She looked at me and said, 'Yeah! I've got a new mummy.' Just a few weeks ago I got Stephanie back and we're now a family again.

I'm so grateful to God for what He's done for me and I love Him so much. He gave me a good family to start with and they've stuck with me even though I didn't deserve it. My sister comes to Preshal so I see her a lot. He's given me Preshal too. And He's given me Stephanie back. I'm so grateful for that. Most of all He's given me Jesus, and that is who has made the change in my life.

Wilson's Story

It's nearly five years ago since I came to Preshal and it has made a big difference in my life. I was a heavy gambler and got into a lot of debt and trouble. My family disowned me because I hurt them so much. My gambling started small, but it didn't stay small. It grew and grew and grew. Eventually it ruled my whole life.

I got into gambling when I was about fifteen years old. I used to spend the weekends with my cousin and when he gambled, I thought I could do the same. I won right away and that was the very worst thing that could have happened. I wasted money on the dogs, on horses and on gaming machines. They are all mugs' games. They eat money. The trouble was that when I won I couldn't walk away because I had to keep trying to win again. And when I lost I couldn't walk away because I had to keep trying to get my money back. It's a vicious circle and once you are sucked in there's absolutely no way out of it.

Although I had a good job, I didn't go home from work on a Friday and give Mum money for my keep; I gambled it all and she often got nothing. I was a real burden to her. I worked to feed the bookmaker, not myself and my family. Then I started selling stuff to get money to gamble. I didn't steal, just did deals to get money to feed my habit. And it is a habit, just as much as drugs or drink. Over the years I lost thousands of pounds. I was the loser. My family were losers. The only winners were the bookmakers, who didn't need my money to make them rich. I was well and truly addicted.

I could gamble two to three hundred pounds in a day. Maybe I would win a hundred, but I'd just lose it again in an effort to win even more. It's a system you can't beat and it just takes over your life. It certainly took over mine. I wasn't brought up to be like that. My family weren't into drink and drugs and gambling. We were well brought up and my two sisters are a credit to the family. While I was gambling I knew I was hurting my family. I loved them and it hurt me to hurt them, but I still couldn't stop. Gambling nearly robbed me of my family, and if you lose your family, you lose everything.

When I saw sadness in my family's eyes I used to walk away with tears in my own eyes, knowing that if I didn't change I would commit suicide. That seemed the only way out of it for me, and the only way to get rid of the problem that burdened my family.

When I first went to Preshal I was hurting so much and I didn't think that anyone in the world could understand. I had heard that they helped people get off addictions and I was so desperate

I was ready to try anything. When I went in I didn't know who were staff members and who had just come in for help. That's what it's like; everyone joins in together. There's no 'them and us'. That day someone told me that I was welcome, that they could help and that they were there for me. It took a lot of courage to go in the door of St Kenneth's Church hall the first time I went to Preshal, but as soon as I was in there I knew I was in the right place. I've come nearly every day since then. It's the place for me and, in a real way, I owe Preshal my life.

Coming to Preshal keeps me busy and away from the devil of gambling from 9 a.m. till 4 p.m., and I am busy: I take part in all the things that are going on and I've learned a lot in under five years. The people who have seen me here see a big difference in my life. One of the things that made me realise I'd changed was that I have money in my pocket! I never had money long enough to put it in my pocket before!

I thought all they would see was a man who liked to bet. I didn't know that people like May could see inside me and could see how miserable and desperate I was. I found new friends, friends who didn't gamble. The staff helped me a lot. People at Preshal are my brothers and sisters and they're so good to me. May's like a second mum to me. It may seem a strange thing to say, but it was her understanding the reality of what it was like to be addicted to gambling that was the beginning of the change in my life. I needed to see what I was really like before I knew what I needed, and it was May who told me how Jesus could supply all my needs. And He has.

Even before I became a Christian, God spoke to me about living with my partner. I knew it was wrong and I proposed to Caroline, asking her to marry me. She said 'yes', and we had our wedding and reception in Preshal. May and the others arranged for a limousine to take us away after we were married. I asked the driver where we were going but he wouldn't tell me. He took us all the way down to a hotel in Ayr for a weekend for our honeymoon! Caroline comes to Preshal and our wee grandson has been coming since he was one week old. He's not there often now as he's at nursery school.

Because I've been a gambler, I think I can help other people who are addicted to betting. I've spoken to a few gamblers, some who bet every single day just like I did, and told them that it is only Jesus who can get them out of the mess they are in. The wife of one man I spoke to told me that he's only gambling twice a week now, and that's a big step for him. She thanked me but I told her to thank God, not me. I've told her husband about Preshal and I hope he'll come and discover Jesus.

It hurts me to see anyone going down the road I went down. People think drinking and taking drugs are killers, but gambling is a killer too. I've known gamblers who committed suicide because of their debts and because of what they were doing to their families. Gambling takes families and splits them up. Bookmakers make money every day of their lives and the only losers are the gamblers. Have you ever seen a poor bookmaker? And they don't care what happens to the people that keep them in their big homes and fancy cars.

Here at Preshal everyone looks out for everyone else. I try to watch for people who are depressed and then I spend time with them and speak to them. If I don't have an answer to what they need, I tell the staff and they find someone who can help. I've seen so many people who come to Preshal changed completely. So many people come in worried and sad and depressed. I don't think many of them had people to talk to. There's always someone to talk to at Preshal.

After I was converted, a friend of the family told Dad and Mum that I'd changed, that I'd become a Christian. They didn't believe it and I don't blame them for that. I'd told them so often that I'd change and I never did. When Dad and Mum realised that I really was different, and that I spent my time trying to help other people, they were really pleased. The Lord has been so good!

Dad and Mum don't spend their evenings sitting worrying what I'm up to now; they can assume that I'm fine. That's a real burden taken off them.

My gambling was nothing to do with Dad and Mum. They are good parents and they brought us up well. My sisters and I went to church until we were about fourteen or fifteen, and I loved going as a child. Preshal has brought me back to that. Now when anyone mentions the name Jesus, it just hits my heart and I'm happy. People even say that I look different now. I have my ups and downs like everyone else. It's not true that life is all roses for Christians, but Jesus is with me and He helps me get through bad times as well as helping me rejoice in good times.

I've gone to places with Preshal that I never thought I'd see. We went over to visit a fellowship in Ireland. That was a wonderful experience. It was great fun and great fellowship too. I'm a singer and we sang a lot while we were there. After I'd sung about the Lord that weekend in Ireland, a man gave his heart to Jesus. I was amazed! Afterwards I went to shake hands with him, but he put his arms around me and hugged me tight. 'I've only known you for a few hours,' he said, 'and now you're my brother, and you'll always be my brother.' That was a great experience. It's hard to imagine that God can use me, a man that lost nearly everything to gambling, to help lead a brother to Jesus!

Gambling nearly cost me my dad and mum and my sisters as well. They would have been better off without me. If I think about it, it makes me really sad what I put them through. But then I think about Jesus, and what He did on the cross for me, and I just can't take in that God so loved the world that He gave His one and only Son that a gambler like me should believe in Him and have everlasting life. That's amazing!

6

Looking at a lost Childhood

Mary Doll's Story

I was born in 1960 and there wasn't enough room in the house for me and my brothers and sisters. We all slept together and there wasn't space to do anything. I was taken into care along with my three brothers and four sisters. I was five then. They all went back home, but I didn't. My mother promised she'd come back for me, but she never came. She said she'd take me home when I was twenty-one, but I never did get home. I lived in children's homes and eventually went to Lennox Castle Hospital (an old-style psychiatric hospital). My family didn't want to know me.

Sometimes I phoned Mum but she just put the phone down.

Years ago I had a good social worker who helped me to find out why I had always been in care. I'd wanted to know that for years. It turned out that my dad had a boyfriend and that was probably why my mum drank a lot. I think that's why we were in care. I used to think it was all my fault, especially when I was the only one of the family left in the home. My uncle wanted to take me to stay with him but my mother wouldn't allow that. I don't know why.

This is how my childhood went. I was in four children's homes and then I was in another hospital before I went to Lennox Castle Hospital. The first home was in Kilmarnock and it was very strict. The last one was Waverley Park in Kirkintilloch. There were about 100 girls there and many of them had big problems. Some of the people who worked there were nice. I liked some but not others. Sometimes when I lost my temper they gave me a jag to knock me out. That wasn't very nice of them. I needed to get away from that place and that's why I started running away. Four or five of us sometimes ran away together but we were always caught and brought back. Once when we ran away I was knocked down by a car. We were punished really hard when we were caught.

On the television you hear terrible things about children's homes. It wasn't like that. I wasn't badly treated, but we could see that other children weren't locked away like we were and that made us unhappy. We just didn't have a life really. It was like being in prison. Though we were clean and fed and looked after, we didn't have a life. That was why we wanted to run away. We were looking for a life, but I was really looking for my family. I always wanted to be back and part of the family again.

I lost everything when I was young, when I was shut up. I lost being young. I was 13 when I started running away. I'd ask people I met if they knew where my dad and mum were and where my brothers and sisters were. They stayed in the Gallowgate in Glasgow and I could get there, but I didn't know exactly where they were. Once I found my mother, but she phoned for the police and I was taken back to the home. Another time when I ran away a man took me up a dark place and raped me. I was just thirteen. I thought he was killing me. I thought all the things that happened to me were my fault. Nobody ever told me they weren't my fault.

People didn't understand. Children's homes weren't really homes. They were just places to put children who couldn't live in their own homes. They weren't happy places. I wasn't happy. For one thing, I didn't know anybody who wasn't in the home. We didn't go out to school and meet normal people. We had a kind of school in the home but we didn't really learn. By the time I was grown up I still hadn't learned to read and write. I knew how to count up but not how to read numbers. I was scared of people outside the home. And after I was raped I was even more scared. It felt as if everyone outside the home was out to get me.

When I was sixteen I took TB and was put in Larkhall Hospital. I wasn't very well then. I was in my twenties, I think, when I went to Lennox Castle. I wasn't in a ward there but in a great big white house behind the Castle. After I'd been there for years they decided that some of us were ready to move into the community. We went into a hostel first but I didn't like that. I'd never been out of care and I was scared in the hostel. I wanted to be out of care, but I didn't know how to do it.

I started drinking when I got out of care. You could meet people in bars and feel like you belonged with them. I always wanted to belong with people and the drink did that for me. Sometimes I drank too much and the police took me in for being drunk and disorderly. Once I was fined for that. I paid my fine by postal order and it went missing in the post. That meant I was in more trouble, and I was put into Cornton

Vale Prison in Stirling and kept there for two nights. When I left they said they didn't want to see me back there again. I didn't want to go back and I shouldn't have been there anyway. I'd not done anything wrong, just my postal order went missing in the post. I only had £54 still to pay of my fine, and that's what they put me in prison for. I said to myself that I'd never be back in prison again.

The hostel didn't suit me very well and I lived in different places after that. About seven years ago I heard from my key worker that there was line dancing in St Kenneth's Church hall and I went along to see what it was about. May came and spoke to me and I discovered I was at Preshal. I told May that I had a drink problem and she said she'd also had a drink problem, but that Jesus had helped her and He could help me too. I started going to Preshal and I was made so welcome. I can still remember what it felt like to go and for people to look up and be glad to see me. May loved me but she was strict too. She told me I'd not to go to Preshal if I had a drink in me. Because I wanted to go to Preshal more than I wanted to drink, that helped me come off the drink.

When I've had slip-ups May has helped me through them. Once I was drunk and disorderly and I was picked up by the police. They took me to the police station for breach of the peace. The next day I told May that I had to go to court and that I was terrified that I'd be locked away again. May helped me through that time. I've been off the drink since then apart from odd slip-ups. One New Year I only drank fresh orange juice and Coke, but then I had one lager and then another one. I didn't mean to do that, but I did. I was really, really sorry for that.

I learned about Jesus in Preshal. May talked a lot about Him and what I most wanted was to see what He looked like. Now I believe in Jesus and I know I have a home in heaven. I'm God's child and He wants me in his home when I die. I don't like the thought of dying, but I'm looking forward to being in God's home. It'll be nothing, nothing like all the children's homes I was in.

God is a real person and He has so much power in Him and so much love. I love to talk to Him and He hears my prayers. I pray for the whole world. Especially I pray for children in homes and for homeless people. It's sad to see people like that in the bad weather. Not long ago a three-year-old girl went missing. Her parents think she is still alive. So I pray a lot for her and I pray for them too. Sometimes I forget to pray for them and then I remember and pray again. I think a lot about that wee girl. She's away from her home and her family, and I was like that though I was in a home. Her parents really want her home again and she doesn't know that.

It's amazing that God answers my prayers. It's amazing that He even listens to me! God's my Father. I love Him to bits and I wish I could see Him. I want to follow Jesus all my life and then go to be with Him in heaven. That will be my new home. That will be my new family. All the people there will be my family. Imagine that! Sometimes I go with May to visit people in their homes and I feel at home there. I feel like part of their family. I love that. Since I became a Christian I have so many people in my life that I can call my brothers and my sisters. I like the feeling of people loving me and caring about me. I used to phone my mum but she would put the phone down on me. That made me really sad. Then I thought, why should I worry about that? I've got a new family now and they love me and want me. My real family are May, Alan and Tracey, Annette and Jim, Irene and Angus, and Sheba, their dog. I don't know why, but they treat me like I'm special.

I saw the film *The Passion of the Christ*. What they did to Jesus was terrible. It was so sad, much worse than anything that ever happened to me. It was amazing that Jesus came alive again after all that happened to Him. It's amazing to think that He did everything for me. I learned a lot from that film.

It's not always easy to be a Christian. There was someone in Preshal who annoyed me pretty badly.

It was just stupid things, but I couldn't take it. One day I was so annoyed I slapped this person on the face. I was banned from Preshal for two weeks for slapping him and it was right to ban me. That made me think about what I'd done. Even when I was banned I was allowed to go and sit outside Preshal and talk to people going in and coming out, and to the ones who came out for a smoke. One day I phoned and asked to speak to someone privately. I broke down and explained that I was very sorry and that I'd never hit anyone before. God helped me, because I didn't go back to the drink then even though I was very upset. I thought a lot about that and now God helps me to look out for the person who annoyed me that day.

Last year the Housing Officer came and told me he had a bedsit I could have. If I didn't like it, I'd have to wait another two years for somewhere else. It's fantastic! It needed a lot done to it but everyone helped. Susan from Preshal came and painted it for me. Jim from Preshal helped me move my furniture. Other people from Preshal did other things to help too, like putting the flooring down. I love having my own home. I get peace and quiet there. It feels great when I sit in my own home with my eyes shut thinking about how much God has done for me.

I didn't ever learn to read and write, but Preshal has literacy classes and I learned to read there. I love reading my Bible, especially about the love of God. There's a fellowship meeting every Sunday night at Preshal and I read the Bible at the meeting. Imagine me being able to do that!

One day May asked me if I would be a volunteer at Preshal. I was really happy to be asked and I said I would. I help the staff out when they are short. If a member of staff asks me to do something, I do it. I don't tell people what to do or anything like that. But if I see someone is upset, I tell a member of staff and they know what to do. I don't ask people their business. If the staff want to talk to someone privately, I move away so that I can't hear what they are saying. There are a lot of volunteers apart from me. We get on well together. I thank God every day for Preshal and for May and for all the other staff. That's my story.

Dear God, please bless Preshal and all the people who go there. Please bless homeless people and please bless children who live in children's homes. And please bless everyone who reads this book. Amen.

7

Looking across the Irish Sea

Tom's Story

More than ten years ago, when May Nicholson was visiting some churches in Northern Ireland, she decided to go to Derry for a day. Derry – or Londonderry, depending on your background – is a very historical walled city. May went on to the city wall and found herself looking down on the Bogside. At that time it was best described as a ghetto. May, being May, decided to go down and investigate. 'Are there any Christians living here?' she asked whoever she met. The Bogside was just not the right place to go looking for born-again Christians, for they were very thin on the ground, but May was pointed in my direction and arrived on my doorstep.

Now, the Troubles in Northern Ireland had resulted in all kinds of do-gooders arriving in places like the Bogside. They came for the day, complete with their own agenda, and left other people to clear up the mess they left behind. So a stranger on my doorstep was not always what I wanted to see. May was different and she completely disarmed me with her honest openness and energy and her burning desire to know what made this ghetto, the Bogside – my home – tick. That day marked the beginning of a friendship, not only between May and myself, but now between Preshal and Wellspring, the Community Church of which I'm pastor.

May could look behind the ghetto and see the people of the Bogside as clearly as she could see the people of Glasgow's Govan. The day we met we shared our stories and discovered that we were both part of what Malachi, in the Bible, called God's 'treasured possession.' The strange thing is that God finds his treasures in very rough places, May in Ferguslie Park and me in the Bogside.

I was born into a Catholic home; every single home in the Bogside was Catholic. And I was young at the time of the Troubles. We had our grievances. For example, if you had a home you had a vote. But three extended Catholic families living together in one house only had one vote, the same as one Protestant student living alone. Feelings ran very high. By the time I was old enough to be aware of what was going on the British Army patrolled the city walls, and gun fights, car bombs and buses on fire were commonplace. In a pathetic kind of a way they were our entertainment. The truth is, there wasn't anything more entertaining in the Bogside than a 'good' ding-dong of a riot.

Children became experts at recognising the sounds of different kinds of gunfire. I could work out which side was where depending on the kinds of guns being used. Once, when I was about eleven years old, I went out to play after my tea. Mum told me to be back by nine o'clock. But before nine o'clock a gun fight had broken out and I was in the thick of it. The British Army was on one side of me and the IRA on the other. I took the line of least resistance and hid behind a low wall with bullets pinging over me. That was when I first realised what strong stuff my mother was made of. Tracer bullets lit the night sky and even the local dogs were silent with fear. Over the noise of the guns I could hear her shouting, 'Tommy! Tommy!' I couldn't do anything about it without risking being shot – and there were children years younger than me who had been killed by then. 'Tommy! Tommy!' her voice went on, only it was coming nearer. When she was near enough to hear me I shouted out to her. And there she was, my wee Maw (every Bogside boy called his mother his 'maw'), marching out between the bullets to take me home. We were no sooner in the door than the ping of bullets was exchanged for a ringing in my ears as she clipped me for being late!

Maw was not put off by bullets or by armed robbers. Once she went down to the little post office at the end of our street to collect her pension and arrived in the middle of an armed robbery. The robbers were behind the counter filling bags with money, stamps and everything else they could lay their hands on. Customers, some of them pensioners like Maw, were lined up against the wall inside the post office. Maw marched up to the counter and demanded her pension – and wouldn't take no for an answer. She'd come for her pension and she wasn't leaving without it. Recognising that he'd met his match, the robber asked her how much her pension was. Maw told him. So, right in the middle of an armed robbery, the robber started to count out her money. 'Do you want your book stamped?' he asked sarcastically, when he handed over the cash. 'I do not!' he was told. 'And I'll be back when the post office opens this afternoon to collect my pension!'

By the time I was in my teens I'd decided that the Catholic faith had nothing to offer me. And, as I didn't meet a Protestant until I was twenty,

I didn't know what they had to offer either. I went off in a search of my own and decided that Communism was the answer, hence my nickname in the Bogside – Commie Tommy. For a while Communism gave me something to live for, but one day I discovered just how empty and hollow it was.

I wasn't far from home when I saw a friend – he was fourteen and I was a little older – going into my back garden with a bomb in his hand. I wondered what he was up to and then saw that some soldiers were going to pass that way and he would get the best lob for the bomb from our garden. Now, I had a big family at home including sisters with their children. In fact, the washing line was full of their nappies. I raced for home but the bomb went off in my friend's hands before he could throw it over the fence. Dashing for the house, I rushed in to see if my family was safe. They were because they'd run for the front door when the bomb went off. Then I looked round the garden and saw my friend with half his torso blown off. The nerves in his body made him sit up and look as if he was holding his hand out in my direction. I just stood there, a statue in a dying hell. People appeared from nowhere and grabbed the nappies to try to stop the bleeding, but my friend was dead. I felt absolutely empty. I knew that I'd no prayers I could say that could have helped him, no absolution to give him, nothing. And I also knew that what I did have – pages of Karl Marx's Das Kapital off by heart – would have done nothing to help him as he died.

Soon after that I headed for Dublin and then London. I went with high ideals and ended up on a building site with a substantial drink problem. Eventually I decided to go to Israel to work on a kibbutz. I could vaguely remember the Bogside community of my very early childhood and I thought I might find a real community once again in a kibbutz. The Israeli Embassy provided the applications; all I needed was a passport. The only problem was that the passport form required signatures from two fine upstanding members of society, and I didn't know anyone who fitted that description. I solved the problem the easy way – by forging two signatures. I hadn't reckoned on the Special Branch arriving at the door and taking me into custody to question me for hours, fool that I was! Before I knew what was happening, I was dispatched back home to the Bogside.

Not long after I returned home there was a knock at my door and two men from an extremist paramilitary organisation asked if I would join them. I said I would think about it for a week and I knew exactly what they were up to. This was at the time when the republicans were placing bombs in England, and these men knew that I was familiar with London and with the transport system there. I could be useful to them, but I didn't know if I wanted to be. Days later, another two men knocked at the door. They were drinking friends and they wanted to know if I would join them at a Christian meeting – strictly to disrupt it, as a Communist, of course! That suited me better and I went along, little knowing the effect it would have on me.

I was still searching after a kind of community and I recognised that these Christians had it. There was something in the way they looked at each other, something in the way they related, something that I couldn't define – but it was the very something I was looking for. I went back to that little meeting myself and became a Christian. Now, I'm an out and out man, so it wasn't long before everyone knew I'd been born again. That didn't exactly make me popular in the Bogside, where to be 'born again' meant to be Protestant, if it meant anything at all. It certainly didn't mean that for me: it meant to be God's man. Soon after my conversion the people at the meeting gave me a Bible, a great big black Bible, and I just loved reading it. But you can't imagine Maw's embarrassment when I went out of the house carrying my Bible. 'Could you not put that thing in a Woolies bag?' she'd say. The strange thing was that she hadn't been in the least embarrassed by my being carried home dead drunk night after night.

One of the first things God seemed to say to me was from Psalm 37:4, 'Commit your way to the Lord; trust in him and he will give you the desires of your heart.' Now, the desire of my heart was for a Christian wife. I was so lonely you wouldn't believe it. You see, for years I was the only Christian in the Bogside, literally. As I travelled around (and God took me to some amazing places) I used to pray, 'Is she here, Lord?' I asked Him that in Russia and Australia, in Romania and America, and in many other countries too. The desire of my heart didn't appear and I kept on praying.

Meanwhile, back in the Bogside a little group began meeting for Bible study. To cut a long story short, the group grew and eventually, in 1994, we became Wellspring Community Church and the people appointed me as their pastor. At home I call myself the caretaker rather than the pastor, as I try to take care of the people. We are neither Catholic nor Protestant and we ask people to leave their sectarian baggage outside the door. We are a Christian group seeking to study God's Word and to apply it to our lives day by day. We are also seeking to be an indigenous Celtic church in our local Celtic community. That has nothing whatever to do with the mysticism that sometimes passes for Celtic Christianity. It's simply all about what Jesus the Lord has done for us. We write our own worship songs, some of them in Irish Gaelic, and all of them based on the Word of God. We use our national instruments rather than an organ.

Our people come from the Bogside and from other parts of the city too. Everyone comes with baggage dating back to the Troubles, whatever side they were on then, and everyone comes with their own baggage of sin. God has blessed us with needy people who know their need and, in His grace, He has reached out to them. I preached so much on the subject of grace that at one point my nickname was Grace Kelly! The Bogside and Govan are different, but there's a sameness too, and the people from Preshal are as at home in Wellspring as we are when we cross the Irish Sea to visit them. God has blessed the many times we've had together with some people becoming Christians as a result.

For the past twenty-five years I've been involved in reconciliation in Derry and I'm one of the three Bogside artists, but that's a long and different story. I finish this short testimony with a smile. I committed my way to the Lord and trusted in Him, and He has given me the desires of my heart. Some years ago the girl next door was converted. I looked for her all over the world and here she was in the Bogside, living quite literally next door! We are now very happily married. I have a lovely step-daughter and we have a great wee boy of our own.

8

Looking at how Preshal works

Cathy's Story

Although I have been involved with Preshal since its inception, I am still taken by surprise by the miracles I see happening there. What thrills me is the constant mending of lives. There are so many goodwill charities that set out to patch up people's problems but Preshal is about mending their lives. I've seen so many people find faith in God, seen their wounds healed and watched as they found a purpose in their lives beyond themselves. There is nothing more thrilling in the whole world than that. For example, I can think of one girl that May met out in the street, a single mother with lots of problems. Now, a few years later, she even looks different. She has direction and purpose. Her eyes are bright and hopeful. If that's the kind of change there is on the outside of a person, it's only a reflection of what has gone on inside their hearts.

I remember once a lady came who had never been before. One or two people grumbled about her, saying that she wasn't very clean and didn't smell very nice. When May heard that, she dealt with it right away, reminding them that once she hadn't been very clean, that in her drinking days she hadn't smelled very nice. Everyone at Preshal knows May's story, and she reminded them that if she had been turned away because of the state she was in, she might never have become a Christian.

I don't mean that members of staff all carry large Bibles around with them and preach at everyone who comes in. It's not like that at all. They meet people where they are. For example, Nancy, whose story begins this book, needed a job and worked first of all as a cleaner. It was some time later that she felt attracted to the Christian faith. Nancy is now on the Board of Preshal. It's so important to have people like Nancy and Ina, both locals who first came for support, on the Board, as they keep us rooted in reality. They know what needs to be done and they help keep our focus on that. It's so easy to have plans that look good on paper rather than plans that are good for people.

To me Preshal is about making people feel valued, precious and great. It's not about the 'leaders' being big fish, thinking how marvellous they are and trying to do good to others. It's quite the opposite. It's about helping other people to discover what God has made them to be, about helping other people to shine. Those who come in the door recognise that Preshal is different and that's what makes so many of them respond as they do.

The thing about making yourself great is that you are never satisfied. Many of my friends are, like me, involved in a number of charities. Each new involvement makes you feel good for a time, but then you have to add more and more as the novelty fades. Having to do with Preshal is just the opposite of that. When I come in the door, I'm just me. I don't think anyone thinks of me as the President or as a duchess, I'm just Cathy Montrose, and that makes me feel good and valued for myself. In a way, what I'm saying is that the welcome I get when I come to Preshal is just the same welcome that is given to everyone else, so I know how they feel.

Being President involves attending monthly meetings, especially just now with a view to raising funds to provide Preshal with a new building. That's a huge project but May always reminds us that nothing is too big for God, and I know she's right. God surprises me over and over again, and He has used May to do that. I was a reluctant speaker but I am much more enthusiastic about it now, at least on the subject of Preshal.

On one occasion May and I were driving to a meeting in St Andrews.

'You can speak first,' she said, when we were more than halfway there.

'I've nothing prepared,' I replied, having not known I was going to be speaking at all, first or second!

May said, 'We'll just have a wee prayer,' and we did.

I wrote a few headings on a piece of paper … and insisted on speaking after she had spoken. When I told someone that story, he asked if I wasn't annoyed with May for putting me in that position. I wasn't, because I felt she was being used by the Lord to test me to trust Him.

May was used to test me that day and I can see Preshal testing those who come to faith in many different ways by giving them things to do, for example, meetings to speak at. The first time I heard Nancy speak at a meeting about what the Lord had done in her life she was in tears and nearly everyone else was too. Her tears spoke even more eloquently than her words did. It seems to me that May is very aware of the temptation to take people for granted. She pushes them so far, but no further. For example, the night she 'made me' speak, she did at least agree to me speaking after her. She has expectations of those who become Christians, but I think she is realistic and sensitive with it. The other members of staff follow her lead in this, as they do in other things too.

Another aspect of my involvement with Preshal simply consists of giving the time to talk with people. We live in a 'busy busy' society where people are so preoccupied with doing, that they don't communicate with each other. Mother Teresa said that one of the ills of western society is that there are so many lonely people.

I want to see the work of Preshal growing because it deals with the fundamental needs of human nature. I believe that as long as it goes on doing that it will grow. It mustn't become more sophisticated and slick. Mending broken lives is a solid rock on which to stand. A lot of theories are just built on changing fashions; they are built on shifting sands. An old hymn puts it like this: 'On Christ the solid rock I stand, all other ground is sinking sand.'

My participation with Preshal is the most satisfying thing I do. I also enjoy it tremendously. While May is deadly serious about the work of Preshal, she's never grim. There's fun wherever May is.

Maclain's Story

'There are two ways to live your life, one is as though nothing is a miracle, the other is as though everything is a miracle.' (Albert Einstein)

To me, what The Preshal Trust stands for can be summed up in two words: passion and compassion. May Nicholson, the staff and the Board of Trustees all have an enormous passion for the work they are doing which is to provide compassion and understanding to everyone who comes through the door. Over 300 have done so since the beginning of 2008, of whom over 100 are young people.

Since May and I set up The Preshal Trust in Linthouse St. Kenneth Church, thanks to the Rev. David Keddie (who gave us the use of his church hall and became an original Board member) and to the many others who gave us great encouragement to start the work, we have moved on apace. Part of our original vision was that those who initially came in looking for help and support, as well as being given the self-belief they needed, would progress to taking responsibility for looking after others. And it was hoped that some might join the salaried staff. This has happened and is ongoing, and others have moved on to employment elsewhere.

We also had a vision to help open up similar projects across the country. Like the ripples on a pond, May and her colleagues have moved out and inspired others using the example of The Preshal Trust and talking about its work at the many engagements to which she and her team are invited. This has also been helped by the sale of May's first best selling book *Miracles from Mayhem*. It's a great read and still available! May describes elsewhere in this book some of the groups she and her team have encouraged to set up and run their own projects. It is her delegation and management skills, amongst her many other talents – not least her sense of humour – which have brought about the remarkable progress of Preshal. She has given her colleagues the opportunity to speak in public and pass on to others practical help on the pleasures and pitfalls of running projects.

It has been just thrilling to have been involved as Chairman since the beginning and to have seen so many lives changed for the better. God has indeed blessed the work and, as May said to me recently, 'Just keep praying and God will show us the way forward as He has done in the past.'

May took a great leap of faith when she began The Preshal Trust, and we are now embarking on another huge one as we plan for new purpose-built premises. As Lloyd George once said, 'You can't cross a chasm in two small jumps'! These new premises are sorely needed, even more so now as another of May's visions is becoming a reality

– a youth group which is being run by her son Alan and a dedicated team. On Tuesday nights they welcome around fifty youngsters and provide them with a variety of activities. It is early days on this project but the potential is immense. Just watch this space!

The new building will require much planning and preparation as our present premises are sorely inadequate. We are indeed fortunate to have on our board Campbell Roxby, an architect recently retired from running his own practice who, as chairman of the building group, is ably assisted by another Board member, Jim McFarlane. As May says, it is what will go on and what will be achieved inside the building that are the most important aspects and not just its exterior façade. Nothing can happen, of course, unless we receive the monies needed to construct and run the building and for this, as always, we rely on the generosity of so many people and organisations. It is brilliant, therefore, that Sir Alex Ferguson has agreed to be our patron for this hugely important step in our progress, a step that will benefit so many more people in Govan and beyond.

Whenever I go to The Preshal Trust I always come away uplifted by all I have seen and heard. There was a memorable day last year when I popped in on official business to be met by an overwhelming reception for my birthday. The kindness, thoughtfulness and humour that went into preparing all the gifts and cards made it quite the best birthday present anyone could have wished for and it is a day I shall never forget. Thanks to May my retiral from business has been somewhat more active, and certainly more meaningful, than it would otherwise have been. For that, and for much else, she has my sincerest thanks.

We are very fortunate to have a splendid Board of Trustees who bring to Preshal their many areas of expertise and it is a great privilege to work with them. When I retire from the chairmanship I hope always to continue to be involved. From the very beginning my wife Jo has been a fantastic support, as has our family. It was Jo who chose the name for the project which sums up so brilliantly all that is being done in The Preshal Trust – making all who come through the door feel precious.

'You must never conclude, even though everything goes wrong, that you cannot succeed. Even at the worst there is a way out, a hidden secret that can turn failure into success and despair into happiness. No situation is so dark that there is not a ray of light.' (Rev. Norman Vincent Peale)

Gavin's Story

MacIain and I have been friends for about thirty years and it was through him that I met May and joined the Board of Preshal. I have a lifetime's experience of business and he felt that my expertise could be of use. My particular remit is fundraising which, with a new building in mind, is quite a remit. Sir Alex Ferguson has agreed to be patron of the building project and we will certainly get some publicity through him, especially as he is a Govan boy himself. The combination of Sir Alex's patronage, May's ability to touch people's hearts, Glaswegian generosity, and the Board's expertise should be a winning one.

When people see real need they are amazingly generous. For example, at the beginning of 2008 we had a Burns' Supper at which various items and skills were auctioned. On that one night alone over £11,500 was raised for the work of Preshal. We are presently preparing a presentation that we hope to take to businesses and trusts with a view to gaining support for the building. Some trusts are not keen to give money to Christian charities, but even they should see the value of the work being done by Preshal.

My wife and I spent a few days in Delhi last year. Despite guide books warning us against it, we allowed ourselves to be picked up by a man with an auto-rickshaw. He was called Ramlal and he was delightful. Ramlal said he would take us on a four hour tour to see the sights. When I asked how much that would cost, he gave me a figure. 'That seems rather a lot,' I said. 'Then let me take you and show you and then you can pay me what you think the tour is worth,' he told us. You can't get fairer than that!

Ramlal took us sightseeing in the afternoon and once again the next morning. In the morning he showed us his Sikh temple. There was a massive pond in front of it with clear water kept clean by catfish. Our guide explained that 20,000 people came to the temple each day to be fed. Then he took us round the back where there were about 100 or more men and women sitting making chapattis – and the women were much faster and better at it than the men! About twenty huge copper containers stood full of curries and thousands of stainless steel plates were being prepared for the people to come for their meal. Anyone could go. Those who were well-off donated money and those who were poor ate freely. It was an amazing thing to see.

Preshal is nothing like that in scale but it is also an amazing thing to see. The doors are open five days a week and on Sunday evenings. People, whatever their need or lack of need, are welcome to come in. Those who are in need of help and support are given it freely by people who really care. That is very beautiful.

May is a visionary, and a visionary who gets things done. I'm a businessman, and it has never been part of my business practice to catch a vision and run after it without first doing the calculations and seeing if the project is viable. May sees what needs to be done and assumes the Lord will provide. He does, but even the Lord is pleased to use Preshal's Board to make His provision. Having said that, there have been times when money has come in when it was needed in a way that can only be ascribed to the good and direct intervention of God. He is full of surprises.

I too have a vision for Preshal, though it may not be the right way forward. I'd like to see it build up some kind of business that would make it self-sustaining. For example, I know of a charity in Liverpool that trained those who came for help in the skills necessary for starting and running a bakery. The money raised through the bakery allowed the organisation's charitable work to continue and grow. Perhaps something like that might come out of Preshal in the future. That's what I would like to see as that would assure its future.

May has a much simpler approach to things. If God wants Preshal to continue, He'll supply the necessary funds one way or another. And that's no pie in the sky thinking coming from her, as I've never met a more practical Christian in all of my life. May's faith affects everything she does. There's hardly a phone conversation that doesn't end with 'God bless you' or with May closing it with prayer. Working with her has been a new experience for me, and it's certainly been an experience I wouldn't like to have missed.

May says

Preshal couldn't do what it does if it weren't for the wonderful staff who work here. Each has different gifts and God has brought all the right gifts, in all the right people, to make up our team. Rena, who is in the office (that's what we call the run-down portakabin that's tucked right beside our building!), has been with Preshal from the beginning. She's had real problems with her health, but she's so committed to Preshal that she has often worked when she should have been at home in her bed. Sometimes we used to play a game – I suppose everyone plays it – 'What would we do if we came into a fortune?' Rena always said that she'd build Preshal a new building. I know she would, for that's where her heart is.

Andy is at Preshal first thing every morning to open up the building. And the earlier people arrive, the earlier he comes to let them in; he's here at 8 a.m. sometimes! He is our handyman, and if something can be done, Andy can do it. He also works with the men who come in, playing pool, going fishing and doing anything else he can turn his hand to. Andy is to be married to Carol in a few months time, and she is part of the Preshal family too.

Kim works in Preshal during the week and also heads up the work in Shotts Prison. She goes out and speaks with me as well, and she's a very good speaker. If Kim were to include her story in this book there wouldn't be a reader with dry eyes. All the hurts she has gone through have given her a heart for reaching out to others, which she does through the work of Preshal.

Eleanor is the quiet one in the team but her meekness is certainly not weakness. She is our découpage teacher and is totally self taught. You should see the work that our people produce with Eleanor and her team's support and encouragement. Not only is she artistic, but she also supports Kim in the work in Shotts Prison. Eleanor and the others just work their socks off, using their gifts and helping others to discover the gifts God has given them. Our prayer is that they will also discover the Lord.

Charlotte is our art teacher, and what a teacher! She started with very raw material, with people who had never painted in their lives but who now produce amazing artwork. People who visit Preshal find it difficult to believe that the paintings on the walls have been done by our own folk. Being creative is so healing for people who come with sore hearts and distressed minds. I think God the Creator works healing in those who make time to be creative. Charlotte gets excited when she sees the work that's done, and so she should!

Tracey is a jack of all trades. She's a trained nursery nurse and she works with the children, especially in our summer programme when the schools are on holiday. She's the kind of girl who sees what needs to be done and does it without any fuss and bother. Alison runs card-making classes and helps in many other ways too. She has just started prison work in Cornton Vale, a prison whose doors have recently been opened to us after much prayer. Annette and I are working there with her.

Preshal has volunteers who love the work and do all they can for it. They like to be called helpers, and that is exactly what they are. They help the staff, they help me and, best of all, they look out for each other. Many have come through the doors with great burdens of their own. If they've been helped with their problems, often the first thing they want to do is to help someone else. Apart from anything else it makes them feel valued, because they know the value of the help they bring.

Every single person in Preshal has a story to tell. You'll read some of them in this book, and a whole book could be written about each one of them. While their stories are all different they have this in common – their hearts are bigger than the River Clyde. They don't just go the second mile, they go the fiftieth mile and still keep going. One of the special things about Preshal is that the volunteers and staff nearly all come through the ranks. That's the best training they could possibly have. I thank God for every single one of them.

Alan's Story

My earliest memories of doing 'outreach work' was going door to door with Challenge magazine round Ferguslie Park with Mum when I was about five years old. I also went to Kairos meetings (a Christian group for recovering alcoholics) with her and they were run along the same lines as Preshal. My memory is that I enjoyed them as much as I see children enjoying coming to Preshal now. The guys who attended Kairos taught me to play the guitar and many other things as well. Church holidays were great fun and practical jokes were the order of the day. I have really happy memories of being a boy in Ferguslie Park.

When I was ten years old Mum was called to work in Mid Craigie in Dundee. I was really sorry to leave Paisley but Mum made sure I got back at weekends to catch up with family and friends. One young Christian man called Cammy, who is now a minister, was like a big brother to me then. Our home in Dundee was always very busy with people coming and going. Folk even came through from Paisley and stayed, especially during the holidays. I can remember there sometimes being twenty to thirty people in our two-bedroom house!

People felt free to come with their problems, many of them needing support to come off alcohol or drugs. Mum welcomed them in and I did too. Sometimes folk ask me how living through that time affected me. My answer is that they should look at the work I'm now doing in Preshal. If I'd not had those early experiences, I don't think I could have understood people as well as I do. I'm never shocked by what I see or hear because I've seen and heard it before. Those years in Dundee also taught me to be thankful for what I have. I saw people reaching the end of the road because of their addictions and that made me very grateful that God saved Mum from that kind of life and gave her a life of service. Knowing all I knew as a boy taught me that I didn't want to go down that route and that I did want to help those who have.

Ferguslie Park, Mid Craigie and Linthouse have the same kinds of problems: poverty, unemployment, social exclusion, drug and alcohol addiction, homelessness, low self-esteem, sin. The Preshal Trust aims to reach out to those who live in the Linthouse area and to help change their lives for the better. Over the years we've seen men and women who were anxious being given peace, people who were unloved being loved, and others who were sad finding joy through the friendship, activities and courses that we provide, and through discovering that Jesus is the only real answer to human need.

My mother has had a vision for the young people of the area for a long time and in April this year we saw that vision begin to become reality. That's when our youth work began and we are excited at the prospect of what God can do. So many of them get into trouble, and very serious trouble, out of plain and simple boredom. Preshal is never boring and we hope to provide activities for the local teenagers that will take up their time and their energy. Of course, we also hope that they will find a new direction in their lives and follow the Christian way.

I qualified as a baker but moved to work with Preshal four years ago, initially as the men's support worker. Recently I completed professional training and I'm now fully qualified for the position I hold within the Trust. I provide advocacy, support and practical activities like model making and fishing and am involved in such things as applying for funding and taking responsibility as needs be. Preshal keeps me busy and I have my own vision for the Trust. I hope that we can make a difference, not only in individual people's lives, but in the whole of Linthouse. The Preshal Trust can help to break the chains of social exclusion and work towards creating a more vibrant community. Our early intervention work with young people is just one step in that direction. Preshal can't change Linthouse on its own but with God all things are possible.

Christine's Story

Preshal is situated in the area of Glasgow which I am most familiar with, having trained in general nursing and subsequently practised as a midwife in the Southern General Hospital in the late 1960s. My six years residing close to the Southern General Hospital in Govan gave me a deep insight into the local culture. Nurses and midwives were treated with kindness and respect and this left me with a lifelong positive impression of Glasgow people – particularly people from Govan.

I do not believe that anything in life happens by chance, I believe it is all predestined. Around 2003, I was approached about helping the work of Preshal. I had never heard of May Nicholson or her work and my contact, John Paterson – who himself has initiated a number of charities in Scotland, not least of them the Princess Royal Trust for Carers – sent me a copy of May's book *Miracles from Mayhem*. Once I started the book I could not put it down and found her story both fascinating and inspirational.

As I have said already, I do not believe any of this was a coincidence since I was already involved in a Glasgow charity called Open Door Trust, both as a trustee and a volunteer. My involvement in this began by a 'chance' meeting with Maureen McKenna and her husband Hugh, who had established the Trust, a Christian charity working in Glasgow City Centre. The main part of Open Door Trust outreach was to women who worked as prostitutes, as well as feeding homeless people and alcohol and drug addiction recovery – a work similar to what May and her staff are doing in Govan. Open Door Trust seemed to be on the brink of expansion when Maureen developed terminal cancer. Having spent a number of years working with Maureen and Hugh, I became very close to her and our outlook in life – particularly our passion for helping homeless people and endeavouring to rescue and rebuild the lives of prostitutes and addicts – brought us very close together on a personal level, so much so that when Maureen's illness got to the point that it appeared there would be no betterment for her, I decided to use my nursing skills and help to nurse her full time in her own home. As I administered whatever Christian support and help I was able to deliver to Maureen on her death-bed, each moment was a great privilege in my life. The irony of the situation was that I received from Maureen and her graciousness as much, if not a lot more, than I gave. The closer it came to her end, the more intense that inspiration and encouragement became, both spiritually and psychologically.

Maureen's life sadly ended at the age of fifty-three on Easter morning in 2002, as did the relationship I had built up with her over three or four years. Nevertheless the memories are lasting and precious. Well over 1000 people turned up at St George's Tron Church, to pay Maureen their last respects, many of whom she had helped to overcome drug or alcohol problems and many more who were homeless people to whom she provided food and clothes as well as care, compassion and Christian comfort.

The police presence and their escort of her funeral cortege, which drove through all the back streets and main streets in Glasgow where she diligently worked with her team of volunteers five or six nights a week for several years, was a testimony to her life on the final journey of her remains, which were laid to rest at Duntocher Cemetery.

The Chairman and Trustees of Open Door Trust, including myself who at the time was the only female on the Board of Trustees, continued to work with passion and vision that we knew Maureen would have wanted. In the intervening period since Maureen's death, and while continuing as both a volunteer and Trustee of Open Door Trust, I found it a tremendous privilege to have been introduced to, and to have an involvement with, Preshal and May Nicholson. Whilst May and Maureen are different in their characters, the synergy between the two of them is quite amazing from the point of view that they were at one time in great need themselves.

After my first few meetings with May it was like my relationship with Maureen all over again and it felt as if I had known her all my life. She was into helping people with all kinds of disabilities, many self-inflicted and others as a result of being victims of the environment in which they were brought up, or pulled into through marriage, or other not unusual circumstances.

One of the first things that impressed me about May was her ability to communicate with people at all levels of society. This skill created a platform of trust on a one-to-one basis and made people whose lives had been a complete disaster in every sense, realise that they had talent and ability but had never been provided with the opportunity or the encouragement to put it into practice. All of a sudden people she rescued, along with her team of volunteers, some of whom were also rescued, were beginning to have a degree of self-respect and confidence about themselves. The cross-section of skills May and her team of volunteers developed – many of whom were at one time in the same social circumstances as those they were now helping – extended to domestic financial management, form filling, cooking, sewing, home baking, literacy and numeracy. This was all built as a result of trust and understanding between human beings who just had a passion to help one another. Lives which had been in a 'lose lose' situation, in a downward spiral, within a short time became a 'win win' situation; as their spirits were raised and their ability to create and achieve was developed at the same time.

What impresses me most about May's work, apart from her ability to give people self-respect, is the love, care and support that she and her volunteers show to those who have lost their way in life and are struggling – some of them to the point of having lost any hope of their life being restored to normality. At the same time as this care and support is shared among them, there is also a spiritual input based on May's belief that if people are changed from the inside out, with a Christian foundation in their lives, the change will be permanent. Their support for children, and particularly for single mothers, is not any less than it is for people who have had ingrained problems – some of them for decades. The overall success of this project is making a huge difference to people's lives in areas where government bodies have failed historically and continue to fail. I have no doubt that if the many people throughout our nation who have come from similar backgrounds to both May and Maureen, and who can stretch funding to amazing lengths, were given more support by national government and local councils, the level of deprivation in our cities and towns would be diminished.

I find it both stimulating and quite amazing that a charity such as Preshal, which really lives from hand to mouth, has no hesitation in handing a bag of groceries to someone in need and even making a donation to another similar charity in a different part of Scotland or Ireland. There are examples where this has happened and where the donation they have given either financially or materially has been equally made up to them through a further charitable donation. It is stimulating and encouraging to watch May's vision in helping to shape similar initiatives in other areas of Scotland and then allow them to fly on their own thereby multiplying the success of Preshal.

Finally, one of the most remarkable experiences I have witnessed at Preshal was where May brought two opposing gangs from opposite ends of Govan Road to a point of socialising together and offering in a unanimous way to support her work. Underpinning all the work which May and her team does is the clarity of her strong faith without which she could not do a fraction of what she is doing, particularly at times when their bank balance is in the 'red' and their challenges and opportunities are not diminishing in equal proportion to their funding.

This is a living example that 'Faith without works is dead' (James 2:17). May's faith is very much alive and you see it clearly manifested in the way she lives and how well she communicates and, at the same time, the amazing amount of work she gets through.

9

Looking at Preshal's People

John's Story

I was five years old in 1941 and that wasn't a good time to be in Paisley. Bombs were a constant danger and people were afraid that their homes would be hit so I was sent off to Dunoon, down the coast and across the water from Glasgow. Auntie Agnes was there and I went to live with her. I vividly remember my first day in St Munns' Primary School, Dunoon, because I cried into a can of plasticine. That's how upset I was at leaving Dad and Mum at home because it felt like a million miles away to a five-year-old, especially as I thought our house would be bombed, and it did suffer bomb damage.

At prayers at the end of my first day in school my teacher said, 'I want you to pray for the lady next door as she has lost her big Irish red setter.' I was only five, but I remember standing there thinking that I didn't know that grown up people could be as stupid as that. She wanted us to pray for a woman who was sad because she'd lost her dog and she'd not even noticed that I was so upset my tears were running into her plasticine tin! Despite my sadness, that was the very first day I felt the comfort of Jesus in my life, and I've known His comfort ever since.

I've always been good with my hands and I'm told I wanted to be a craftsman since I was seven years old. But I was brought up in a divided society. My family were Catholics and in the West of Scotland in those days Catholics and Protestants didn't mix, and Catholics didn't become craftsmen because they couldn't get apprenticeships. But things were changing, maybe because of the war, and a girl in my class became the first Catholic to be employed in the Commercial Bank of Scotland, and I also remember when the first Catholic girl got a job in the Bank of Scotland. It's hard to believe how different things are just sixty years later.

My dream of training as a craftsman came true and I served my apprenticeship as a coach trimmer, which was, even then, a dying trade. After two years in the Army in Aden, I went back to my old job. It was secured for me during my Army service. Within a week I was being bullied by my foreman. He wanted me to work on Sunday, being paid double my hourly rate, even though there wasn't any work for me to do. I had no choice. I went in, worked at whatever I could find to do and then put my notice in the following day. But what to do next?

As I said, I've always been good with my hands so I opened up a tiny upholsterer's shop in Paisley. Of course, the Catholics supported me and enough money came in to keep the family. I got some big jobs to do, and I really do mean big, like making the biggest curtains in the country for Rank Organisation! God really blessed us and eventually I had three shops all working full-out. But in 1976, a year of industrial upheaval and three-day working weeks, people couldn't afford to buy carpets etc., even when I struggled on trying to sell them by candlelight! I went out of business, lost our home, and with my wife and seven children moved to a council house in Renfrew.

After some time the children started complaining about sleeping on the shelves in pokes (sleeping bags). Then my wife said that there was a house for sale at Bishopton that we should go and see. 'We can't afford it,' I said. But the family insisted and we went to see it. It was a complete and total wreck even though it was in a very nice place. 'I'll give you £12,000 for it,' I told the man who was showing us round. He looked at me and shook his head. The seller had inherited the house. I think the only reason that he hoped for a sale was that he lived in Tasmania and had never seen the state it was in! Two hours later I was told I could have it for £12,000. My boys and I did up that house without the help of a single tradesman, and my wife and I are still in it today.

I'm an inventor and I've made all sorts of things from glass roofs that you can walk on to a chair that commemorates the holocaust. God gave me the gifts I have and I've always tried to use my gifts to serve Him. That's why I come to Preshal and do what I can here. I was brought up in a Catholic home and I love the Lord Jesus and worship Him because He died for me. The people who come in to Preshal are Catholics, Protestants and nothing at all. There's not the same divide in Glasgow nowadays because so few people go to any church. It doesn't matter to me what church people go to, I just want to do what I can to help them because God's given me the gifts to do that. What I do for Preshal, I do for Jesus. I love Preshal and May and I serve them any way I can.

Lil's Story

I was born and brought up in Govan, not far from where Preshal is now. Dad and Mum lived in what was then known as Wine Alley. Dad was an alcoholic and Mum had TB. We lost our home and Gran brought me up. Gran encouraged me to go to church (I was from a Catholic family) though I went to meetings in different churches. I was even on Songs of Praise on television when I was nine years old. I left school with one O level and was told I'd not amount to much.

My partner and I had a daughter when I was twenty-one. When our daughter was seven I was expecting again and we got married. He was using drugs and he also had mental health issues. My world focussed on the new baby coming and then I miscarried. I think I had a kind of breakdown. Two years later we had another daughter, but by then my husband had schizophrenia.

For the next couple of years I was just a bag of nerves. I was on my own with two young girls, scared and teetering on the edge of another breakdown. By the time my younger daughter was about three I decided to do something for myself and I did a course through the local development company. I enjoyed the course so much that I stuck in and eventually went to university and got a degree. When I graduated I thought my worries were over. I wish they had been. I was eight months pregnant when I graduated and could only get sessional work for a year but then I found a permanent job.

My then partner was also a regular cannabis user and what should have been a good time was really very hard. We were together for six years. When he left, our daughter was three years old. I had a whole bundle of worries: three kids, no income, depression and bankruptcy. It took me four years to stop blaming myself, and that's when I met May. Eventually God led me to Himself and I was born again. I thought things would get better then but the next six years were the worst years of my life. I only got through them with God's help.

Now I'm a sessional worker at Preshal, especially helping with the youth work. I'm looking for other employment as I need to work full-time. But whatever job I get, I'll take what I've learned at Preshal with me and use it there. God has used Preshal to help me and bless me. Most recently He has been teaching me about patience and endurance, and I've still a lot to learn about both. I hope He'll use what I've learned to help others and bless them too.

Grace's Story

I didn't have a happy start to life. My dad took a pint every night and Mum called him an alcoholic and divorced him. That was bad, but it only got worse. Mum remarried and my sister and I were sexually abused by our stepfather and his two brothers. I reported what was happening but Mum made sure the charges were dropped. I was abused right until I left home. The strange thing was that my stepfather drank wine morning, noon and night and Mum stuck with him. I hated my mother.

Life was horrendous and I would just love if no-one else went through what I went through, but it's not like that. I ended up abusing myself, taking overdoses, being put in padded cells and given electric shock treatment. If anyone reading this is being abused as I was, don't let it go on until you end up like me. Please don't stay silent. Go for help before you're locked away. Speak out and get help. I want to shout that out so that people can hear me. It's so important.

I moved to stay with my granny and then went to work in hotels to get right away. But I didn't always manage to work and sometimes spent long times in psychiatric hospitals. When I was working in a hotel I met Alan and he asked me to marry him after we'd been going out for three weeks. We've been married for thirty-seven years now. Alan has put up with a lot, and he didn't know the half of what had happened to me because I just couldn't talk about it. He even came with me when I went to see a psychologist because he wanted to understand and to help. I've a lot to be grateful for.

For years I was deeply depressed. I didn't clean or cook – even though I'd worked as a cook in a hotel. Sometimes my depression went into a downward spiral and I was in despair. Alan stuck by me though it was hard for him to see me like that. For a time I went five days a week to hospital just to get out the house. Then I was sent to a mental health place where we were given things to do. But all we did was play bingo and cards so I stopped going. That wasn't helping me at all. Then I went to another mental health group where they were doing découpage and I liked that.

My community worker at the time knew about Preshal and that they were doing découpage there and she suggested that five of us in the mental health group went along to Preshal. I thank God for the first day I went in the door of Preshal and I've never looked back since then. I even went to my psychiatrist and told him that I wouldn't be going back to mental health groups. My doctor sees the difference in me, as does Alan and the family. I don't self harm now and I don't mope about in bed all day.

Going to Preshal changed me because I became a Christian. I gave my heart to the Lord and He took away my broken heart and gave me a new heart. It was very strange how God brought me to believe in Him. May often goes out to speak at meetings. She's a great speaker. One night she was going to Largs and she asked me to go with her.

'Are you from Paisley?' an old lady of ninety asked me.

'No,' I said. 'I'm originally from Possilpark.'

She looked at me.

'I remember you,' she said, 'and I remember your granny.'

I looked at the old woman.

'You used to come to my Sunday School in Possilpark,' she said. 'And I remember the wee girl who came with you.'

She was right enough! All these years later that old lady remembered me. It was amazing. I didn't remember her, but she remembered me.

At that time I was taking over forty pills a day just to get through each day and I was always shaking. But that old lady remembering me did something inside me. I can't explain the feelings I had. It was as though my heart was melting. The next week Tom Kelly from Northern Ireland came over to Preshal, and I gave my heart to the Lord. That night Tom told me that I had to tell people that I was a Christian. I've done that. I've even gone out with May when she's been speaking at meetings.

I used to curl up in bed and wish the days away; now there aren't enough hours in the day. I'm at Preshal every day and I just love helping there. What a change in my life. It's like darkness changing to light. I don't want to say any more about what happened to me, I'd much rather talk about the Lord and about what He's doing in the lives of the people who come to Preshal. A lot of them went through the same kind of things as I did and Jesus can save them too. I'll tell you what a change there has been in my life – God has even helped me to forgive my mother.

Libby's Story

Last year I received a letter from the Home Office that gave me a terrible shock. It was to say that the man who murdered my young brother was being let out of jail. He had not only killed my brother but a prison officer as well. That letter took me right back to when I was five years old. My young brother was just four, and my mum and I found him. Mum took ill shortly afterwards and I had to look after her. I don't think I was ever a child again. Despite what happened, or maybe because of it, Mum brought up four boys as well as her own family. She was just a wee woman, and when the boys were bad she made them sit down on a stool to give them a row or punish them.

Mum remarried, and the man she married turned out to be my wicked stepfather. He was abusive, both physically and sexually, until I was eighteen years old, when I left home to train as a nurse. He was especially bad to me when Mum was in hospital having their children. A few years later I met Andrew and we married and had Jacqueline. God only gave us one child, which was maybe just as well. Mum developed breast cancer and, between looking after her and Jacqueline, I think Andrew felt shut out. Whatever happened, our marriage broke up and I found myself a single mum.

My mum brought up my sister's son, and he was still a boy when she took cancer. 'I'll live till Alexander's fifteen,' she told me, and she died on his fifteenth birthday. I was with her that day. She fell and I helped her up and took her to the bedroom. I asked Mum what had happened. 'Pet, I don't know,' she said, and then she stroked my hair. Mum wasn't a touchy-feely person, and those were the last words she spoke and the last thing she did. She died in my arms. It was terrible.

Exactly a week after that my stepfather died too. He'd been working in a big drum and had inhaled some kind of gas. He was ill for a while and then died. I wasn't sorry he was away but it broke my heart to see Mum's grave opened up again. And it made me so angry that that brutal man's body was right there beside her. When I lost my mum, I lost my best friend. When I lost my stepfather, I lost my worst enemy. Jacqueline was in her own flat by then but I still had Alexander to look after. Although I loved him like my own, I was totally empty inside after Mum died, empty of everything except anger. My nerves were shattered and it was really hard to go out of the house. For the next two years my life was a total mess.

I used to get up in the mornings so depressed that I was scared of the day ahead. Sometimes, when I tried to go out the door, I just had to turn round and come right back in. I was so scared, though I didn't know what I was scared of. Jacqueline did my shopping for me. Eventually the doctor referred me to a psychiatrist, a lovely young woman, who came to see me at home. She spent ages explaining to me that there was nothing outside that was going to hurt me. After a while she went outside with me and gradually we went further and further. I remember the first day I went into a shop again and how terrified I was. I couldn't go on a bus or anything like that.

It was after that that I met May outside Preshal, which was then meeting in St Kenneth's Church hall. She talked to me and seemed a really nice person. When she invited me in I discovered they were doing découpage. I'd never seen that before. In découpage you get a sheet with several copies of the same picture, all a bit different from the others. You cut round them and then stick them on top of each other to give a 3D effect. I joined in and cut round pictures as if there was no tomorrow. I was so nervous being out of the house, and so nervous of being in a new place, and so nervous of people I didn't know, I found I could shut them all out of my mind if I concentrated on cutting round these tiny complicated pictures.

After a while I started to talk to the other people who came to Preshal. When some of them talked about abuse they'd suffered I felt all screwed up inside. My way of coping was to shove things to the back of my mind. I did that with everything. For example, my stepsisters didn't know about my brother's murder. Even Jacqueline didn't know, and she certainly didn't know about my abuse. It was all locked up inside me and I couldn't let it out. I suppose that was one reason I missed Mum so much. Although she never knew (so far as I know) about the sexual abuse, she did know about the beatings. She couldn't help but know, as some of the beatings were to save my stepfather from beating her.

Hearing about other people's problems at Preshal brought everything back and I started having flashbacks. But the thing about Preshal is that it's a safe place. I think that's what makes Preshal different from anywhere else I've ever been. It's a safe place. I don't think anyone who hasn't been seriously depressed will understand what I'm trying to say. The truth is, that if it hadn't been for May, if it hadn't been for Preshal, I don't think I'd be alive today. Jacqueline agrees with me and she's very thankful to May too. I couldn't have asked for a better daughter. She has a good job and is doing really well. Alexander has a family now and they are all doing fine. Mum would have been proud of her family.

Since I've come to Preshal even my doctor has seen the difference in me. I don't mean that everything is back to normal, but life's a lot more normal than it used to be. May keeps pushing me to do things, like going out in a crowd. I still find that hard. But she pushes gently and I manage to do things I don't think I can do until I realise I've just done them! There's an outing coming up soon with Preshal. I said I'd not go as I'd just hold other people back but May didn't let me off with that. She said that we'd just work round what I was able to do. Now I'm quite looking forward to the time we'll spend together.

Preshal is like a family to me. I try to help people and they are there when I need them. And I sure needed them when that letter came from the Home Office saying that my wee brother's murderer had been set free. I know he's living not very far away and that's a huge burden to me. I just hope and pray that he doesn't hurt another child. Some of the people in Preshal know my worries, but I don't talk about them a lot.

I come to the Preshal fellowship meeting on Sunday evenings and I really enjoy that. It gives me a good feeling to be there. I listen to the worship and can associate with it a lot of the time. But it's the day-by-day Preshal that means most to me. It's there for me Monday to Friday and I'm there for whoever comes in. Helping as a volunteer gives me a reason for being here, but the biggest reason is that Preshal is a family unit and I am part of the family. I have my ups and downs; sometimes the 'ups' are higher and the 'downs' are lower than others, but they are there for me. May is always there for everybody. God has given her a very big heart.

Jimmy and Janet's Story

Both of us have Christian backgrounds, though there have been times in our lives when we've not been shining as brightly for the Lord as we try to do now. Despite that, God has been very good to us.

Jimmy – I became a Christian when I was sixteen years old and fishing down at Yarmouth. I was shipwrecked three times in my career at sea. The first time was on my seventeenth birthday when we were heading out to the North Sea fishing grounds in fog and an Aberdeen trawler cut us in half. Sliced boats don't float, and we went down in four minutes. The next time we were heading back to Oban, again in fog, and without radar, when we went ashore on Sheep Island. And the third time the boat had been in Campbeltown for a re-fit. After rounding the tip of Kintyre we were shipwrecked on the notorious Mull of Kintyre and had to climb up 700 feet high cliffs to safety. The coastguards met us at the top! I believe that the Lord kept me safe because He had work for me to do.

Janet – I also became a believer when I was young, but fell away. Sadly, it was some years before we came back to our first love of the Lord, and we are now redeeming the years we lost.

Jimmy – I retired in 1999 and immediately began helping Moldova Ministries. This involved collecting clothes, furniture and anything else that might be useful, storing them in our garage until there was a van load, and then taking the things to a store some miles away where they were kept until they could be taken to Moldova. We are so rich here and we don't realise it until we see how people in some countries live. Having said that, I've seen those with hardly anything in their homes show more contentment than we do with all our wealth.

Janet – For a time I ran a charity shop that raised funds for community work being done by our own church, the Southside Christian Fellowship in Ayr. Moldova Ministries and Preshal also benefited from the shop. We both felt that we'd been blessed with health and energy in our retirement and we wanted to serve the Lord as best we could.

Jimmy – After a time we were no longer able to send furniture and clothes, etc. to Moldova, and we started bringing things up to Preshal, where May was always able to use them. For a time we brought up a van load every Thursday and then delivered it to people who needed it wherever in Glasgow they lived. We sometimes furnished whole flats for people who had been allocated them but who had nothing to put in them.

Janet – Jimmy was at sea much of our married life and we are really enjoying doing things together in our retirement. I hope what we do at Preshal is helpful to other people; it's certainly a blessing to us.

Jimmy – Four and a half years ago I developed cancer. Having come through that, I feel that the Lord must still have work for me to do. We come to Preshal on Thursdays and spend much of the day just chatting to people. So many want to talk, and we often talk about the Lord. I don't force the conversation round to Christian topics. Somehow Preshal is an easy place for people to talk about Jesus. I'm sure that's in answer to prayer.

Janet – I get involved in art and crafty things, doing things in the kitchen and sometimes playing with children. We are grateful to the Lord for allowing us the blessing of serving Him through Preshal.

Lindsay's Story

I was born into a good home in the Govan area of Glasgow in 1950. My family went to church and we were raised with Christian values. I didn't think seriously about religion until I saw our youth leader being baptised. Our Methodist church only ever had infant baptisms, and that was the first adult baptism I had seen. That really set me thinking.

Around that time I saw Cliff Richard on television discussing his faith. I was intrigued. When Cliff came to Glasgow my girlfriend, who was also a fan, got tickets for a small meeting he held in a church hall. We enjoyed the gospel songs and, when he began open discussion, I was surprised to find myself first on my feet asking him how I could be a good Christian. He told me, 'It's not about rules; it's about getting to know Jesus.' It was as though a light switched on inside me and my journey began. That happened thirty-eight years ago.

I went to college to study Youth and Community Work. While I was there my interest in music took me into bands. In the 1970s I was in a glam rock band, complete with glitter and platform shoes. That lifestyle presented many temptations, but God never left me. He promises never to leave us or forsake us, and He keeps His promises.

When I met my wife-to-be we were so much in love that I was convinced that God had brought us together. All sorts of things seemed to confirm that to me. Sadly, marriage isn't as simple as that and, though we felt we were meant for each other, the realities of keeping a house, earning a living and coping with children, didn't come easily to us. Over the years frustrations, anxiety and bitterness crept into our relationship. We weren't aware of it then, but Satan was slowly destroying the good gift we believed God had given us.

It wasn't until we started attending the Victory Christian Centre that we found some stability. We were given strength to meet our difficulties and we also saw God doing wonderful things in the lives of those we loved. For example, Mum suffered from agoraphobia and couldn't leave the house. Even in the safety of her own home she was afraid to be alone. At first we were sympathetic, praying for her and giving her tapes and Bible verses to encourage her, but all to no avail. Then one morning I woke with a righteous anger in me. I was furious at Satan. I rebuked the tormenting spirit that was ruining Mum's life ... and the following Sunday she was in church! Before long she was ministering to others with problems.

I've been playing music, singing and writing songs since my schooldays, and have led worship in churches for years because I can hold a tune. But holding a tune and worshipping are different. The most powerful experiences I've had when leading worship have been when I've lost confidence in myself and cried out to God for help. Of course, the other element of truly spiritual worship is that the worshippers are of one accord and focussing on Jesus.

One day I was alone in church praying. The large lectern Bible was lying open at Matthew 6. I felt led to take the Bible to the piano and then it seemed as if a song unfolded before me. Shortly afterwards I played it at a women's conference and the whole place was in tears, including me. Here are the words, taken almost directly from God's Word.

Therefore I say don't be anxious for your life
or for the food you eat.
Don't be anxious for the clothing that you wear,
my Father meets your needs.
Behold the birds of heaven; they will never sow
neither will they reap.
My Father feeds them well, and don't you know
you are worth much more than these.
Consider all the lilies of the field,
consider how they grow.
They do not labour sitting at a spinning wheel;
they let their beauty flow.
Yet I say to you, even Solomon the king
in all his glory
was not arrayed as one of these small things.
But you are worth much more than these.

That song talks about not worrying and it seems to speak to those who hear it. It speaks to me too, for lately I've struggled with my faith and my direction, and my marriage has broken down. The problems come when I depend on people and on my own strength to bring happiness. I need to relearn my dependence on the Lord.

So many of those who come along to Preshal, some without any Christian background at all, come to faith in Jesus. When they do so, they show such humility and gratitude that their sins are forgiven. The atmosphere is so non-threatening, so homely, that they can share their experiences freely. I hope I contribute something when I go to the Tuesday youth nights and the fellowship meetings on Sundays. Being at Preshal certainly helps me, and I trust that God will use it to support me through this present difficult stage of my life.

10

Looking North to Kilmallie

Kiki's Story

When I was a student for the ministry, a friend suggested that I go and visit Preshal. I'd never heard of it, but I was spending some weeks on placement in a church in Glasgow and decided to go along. There was a lot happening, including a small group of people who were gathered for Bible study. I was asked to speak to them and to give my testimony. May said afterwards that I was lucky that some didn't get up and leave the room when I said I used to be a policeman! Maybe she was joking!

I became a Christian in 1983, when I was twenty years old. I read a book by Spurgeon on

God's mighty works that said that when God did mighty works, He didn't use mighty people, so I thought He might use even me. I wanted to spend my life serving God but I didn't know what He wanted me to do, and I certainly didn't feel like a mighty person. It might seem strange but I just couldn't think of any other 'Christian job' except the ministry, and that didn't feel right for me, at least at that time. I sent away for leaflets about various colleges and then settled on the idea of the police service. There was no place in my mind for the idea of a police 'force'; I saw the police very much as the police service. Working in the police seemed to me to be a way of serving people.

Although some people seem to think it, I'm not really a very confident person and that affected the kind of police work that I felt comfortable doing. Eventually I went into community liaison / crime prevention and that suited me very well. I was dealing with the public, mainly in areas involving drug and alcohol abuse. I was in the police service for seventeen years and felt I was doing a good job. Despite that, I knew deep down inside me that, even if I could fix all the problems I was meeting day by day, that would not hit at the heart of the problem. I was meeting the symptoms, and sometimes could do something to help, but the problem was sin and that was way outwith the remit of the police service.

Five years of my police service were spent in Fort William and it was there that I met Anna Cunningham, who was to become my wife. In 1989, when we were going out together, I remember us walking along Loch Linnhe discussing our future. We agreed that what made us tick was being close to the Lord, and that when we drifted from the Lord we just didn't tick at all. I can honestly say that it was our hearts' desire to walk with the Lord and to serve Him all our days. It never once crossed my mind that fifteen years later we would find ourselves back in Fort William, and that I would be a minister there. God works in strange ways!

I had always been concerned about people with alcohol problems. I don't think you can be brought up in the west of Scotland without being aware of the devastation that drink can bring in the lives of individuals and their families. Personally, most of my greatest regrets are due to my drinking. I didn't have to drink much for it to affect me badly, but I didn't have the sense to avoid it altogether. In fact, I had a fear of becoming an alcoholic. But my experience means that when I meet people with drink problems, my heart goes out to them in empathy. I do know what they feel like, but I also know that the Lord Jesus who saved my soul can save their souls too.

From Fort William I was transferred to the Isle of Lewis, and then I applied for a move south to the Isle of Uist. We had heard that there was a good Christian work going on in Uist under the Free Church minister, Iain MacAskill. We hoped when we went there that we could become involved in the congregation, especially in the work it was doing with people with addiction problems. Having applied for the transfer, nothing seemed to happen for ages. I had told a Christian colleague about our hopes and he sent me a compliment slip with the reference 'Jeremiah 29:11' on it. I didn't look up the verse at the time … and then lost the piece of paper. One Sunday afternoon, during that waiting time, our daughter Mairi (she was four years old) came into the room with the piece of paper in her hand! I looked up the Bible to see what the verse said and God really spoke to me as I read, "'For I know the plans I have for you," declares the Lord, "plans to prosper you and not to harm you, plans to give you hope and a future."'

Iain MacAskill came up to Stornoway to visit his father in hospital and, knowing our hope of a transfer to his part of the world, he came to see us. He held worship in our house and read the following passage from the Bible:

'Then the word of the Lord came through the prophet Haggai: "Is it a time for you yourselves to be living in your panelled houses, while this house remains a ruin?" Now this is what the Lord Almighty says: "Give careful thought to your ways. You have planted much, but have harvested little. You eat, but never have your fill. You put on clothes, but are not warm. You earn wages, only to put them in a purse with holes in it." This is what the Lord Almighty says: "Give careful thought to your ways. Go up into the mountains and bring down timber and build the house, so that I may take pleasure in it and be honoured," says the Lord.' (Haggai 1:5-8)

That really did speak to Anna and me. We were living in a nice house, with a beautifully panelled hallway right enough. And it was certainly true that the money we earned seemed to pour out through holes in our pockets. God seemed to be telling us clearly that we should move to Uist and help Iain with building up the church there. Apart from building up the people (and the church is people, not stones and mortar), his small congregation was virtually rebuilding the church.

The transfer came through. We were on the move and I started work on a Monday morning. The following Saturday evening I found myself at a Road to Recovery meeting where the speaker was Maureen McKenna, who worked with some of the most needy people in and around Glasgow city centre. Maureen and her husband Hugh, both converted alcoholics, made a huge impression on me. In fact, that evening Maureen prayed for me as I had never heard anyone else pray for me, and I have never forgotten her prayer.

Our denomination was going through a difficult time just then and, in the emergency that resulted from it, Iain asked me if I would preach the following Sunday! Somewhere in the back of my mind there had been the thought that one day I might find myself in the pulpit, but that time always seemed years in the future. God, however, has His ways of working and I preached for the first time within a fortnight of arriving in Uist. That certainly pinned my colours to the mast. I was the new policeman on the island, and the new preacher too! There was a kind of exhilaration in that situation for me, but it was unsettling for Anna. After all, we'd just unpacked our bags in a Uist police house. Was God wanting us to pack them all up again and move to Edinburgh to train for the ministry? It was all too much and too quick for her at the time.

Congregational life in Uist was wonderful and my work was too. Some members of the police service were converted, and we used to joke about it being revival time. Once, when there was a revival in Barvas on the Isle of Lewis, newly converted Christians went to the police station and handed themselves in for breaking the law in the past, sometimes many years before! We didn't quite see that in Uist.

In a small island community everyone knows what everyone has done, sometimes before they've done it! I visited a fellow who binged on drink, and he was the worse for it when, still in uniform, I went to see him one day. The place was full of dirty dishes and I washed up before I left. A month or so later I was called out to a disturbance. After things had quietened down a bit I made for the door. 'Are you not going to do my dishes?' a voice called. I think my binge-drinking friend had been talking, I certainly hadn't! I felt a little foolish, but only for a while.

Our next move was from Uist to Edinburgh, and from service with the police to training for the Free Church of Scotland ministry. By God's time for us to move, Anna was at peace about it and totally supportive. Anything I've been able to do has been done because she has been right beside me. We're a team. It was when I was in my second year at College that I made my first visit to Preshal. I'd never met May before, but I realised right away that she was doing the same kind of work as Maureen had done before her early death. I felt at home.

That day there were little groups of people all doing their own things. Some were playing snooker, others doing craft work, and some sitting talking, as well as the little group I spoke to. There was a happy and relaxed atmosphere. One of the folk I spoke to was called Sandra, and she told me that her husband had been murdered and she was left with two girls. I thought, this is where the rubber hits the road. This is where the gospel needs to be shared. My passion is to live the Word and share the Word, and I felt so at home because that's exactly what Preshal seemed to be doing.

For the remainder of my training for the ministry my thoughts kept returning to Preshal, and to the poor and needy parts of Scotland's cities. I could picture myself ministering in a place like Govan. God's plan was different, but God's plans are always perfect. Instead of working in an inner city, Anna and I found ourselves in Kilmallie, just down the road from Fort William, where we had met all those years before!

Back in our Uist days I'd met Stan Gowdy, who had been an alcoholic. Stan was converted through Staurus, the same organisation God used to bring May to Himself. We met again when I'd finished College, and was considering the call to Kilmallie. 'You're just the man for Kilmallie!' he said. 'There's a group in Fort William who are interested in Staurus work and it needs leadership. You're just the man!' That was one of the ways in which God showed me where my ministry should begin. When we were settled there, Stan came to speak, and it seemed that God was opening the door for a work with people with addiction problems. At first we met monthly, but a month is too long if you need that kind of support and we moved to meeting fortnightly. Then one of the men who came along was found dead in his home. That spoke to us of the urgency of the need and we moved to a weekly meeting. Now we meet every Monday and recently we've begun meeting on Tuesdays at lunchtime as well. We call ourselves Road to Recovery, and it's a road that will last a lifetime.

Hugh and Maureen McKenna were totally up-front about the fact that their help was Christian help. May is exactly the same at Preshal. There is no pretence that Christianity is an add-on. That's what Preshal is about. And May's support of the work at Kilmallie has helped us to keep the same focus. That is vitally important and it takes me right back to my policing days just down the road in Fort William when I realised that even if I could fix all the problems I was meeting day by day, that would not hit at the heart of the problem. The heart of the matter is that sinners need a Saviour, whether they are alcoholics or fine respectable and upstanding members of our sinful society.

On Monday evenings we have a welcome and then a time of prayer for those who are there and for others who normally come and who have not turned up. That's followed by a talk based firmly on the Bible. Sometimes a converted alcohol-ic shares his testimony, or sometimes we have a testimony from a person who has never been troubled by drink at all. The key to the work is that it is up-front. There is no pretence. We are not offering soup, sandwiches and sympathy. We are offering Jesus Christ as Saviour and Lord. Not all who come along are alcoholics; some have addictions of another kind and others suffer from depression or other mental health issues. Some just know they are in need. Not only are the problems different; the people come from vastly different places. It's hard to believe, but away in remote Kilmallie we have people from various parts of mainland Scotland, the Western Isles and even Spain and Portugal coming along! This is not my work alone. I receive a tremendous amount of support from Ronnie, a former alcoholic and now a devoted Christian, who has a tremendous heart and burden to share the gospel with those in need.

One person who came along on a Monday evening was Lachie. At that time he was struggling with addiction, depression and a broken marriage. Shortly afterwards he asked about coming to church and bringing his girls to Sunday School. Since then Lachie's life has been turned around. He was baptised along with his three girls and is now a member in our congregation. He uses his skills as a chef by helping with catering in the church, and he is growing in his faith and understanding of Jesus, his Lord and Saviour.

There are a lot of miles between Preshal and Kilmallie, but that doesn't prevent May coming up here to encourage us in the work we are doing. Part of her vision is to see groups all over Scotland, not run by Preshal, but run by Christians with a passion for reaching out with the Gospel to those who need it, and every single man, woman and child comes into that category. One day recently we had twenty-eight school children visiting the church and we gave them juice and biscuits outside in the sun. The following week we had our Road to Recovery folk outside the church having their soup and rolls in the sun. We also have Evergreens, a lunch club for older people. A lovely thing happened at Evergreens – one of the young helpers became a Christian!

I'm not a one-man band. Anna's not behind me, she's right beside me, and often ahead. She is an amazing support and I couldn't do what I do without her. She also does a great deal in her own right. Our children, Mairi, Donald and Sine, bring such joy and fun to our family. They help make the difficult days good days! The congregation here is also hugely supportive in all the different aspects of the work of serving God in this community. I knew that when I started hearing the different parts of the congregation's work being prayed for at our weekly prayer meeting, and prayed for meaningfully and from the heart.

11

Looking from even further Afield

Manu's Story

My wife and I were brought up in Christian families in South India. We moved to Scotland because of my work. God has always led and guided us and we believe that it was He who brought us to Glasgow and who introduced us to May and to Preshal. Our daughters are very much at home in Preshal, especially Elaine who is eight years old. She is very musical and she sometimes helps lead the worship at the Sunday fellowship meeting.

How God gave us our two daughters is quite remarkable. Elaine might easily have died at birth because she had the cord wrapped twice around her neck. But God spared her to us and we always thank Him for her. Then we waited a long time for Evelyn, our second daughter to be born. My wife Ann, did not become pregnant and the doctors were not able to tell us why. Finally it was decided that she should go for an operation to discover the cause of the infertility. As I drove Ann to the hospital I was praying that, whatever happened, God would be given the glory. I was troubled in my mind as our family was putting pressure on her to have this surgery, and she and I had already postponed it several times. In our culture we respect our parents in such a way that, even when we are adults and married, we try to do as they say. When we arrived at the hospital the doctor did a test and then came back twenty minutes later to tell us that Ann was pregnant! That is why we say that both our daughters are miracles for us.

A friend, who is a leader in prison ministry, brought me to Preshal and that's how I met May for the first time. I was interested to see Preshal and to learn what it was about. Both Ann and I really like what is done here. We feel it is what the church should be doing everywhere. The staff members try to show the love of Jesus rather than go through rituals and traditions. Outside Preshal, if you see a drunkard, you might fear him or try to avoid him. Inside Preshal people look for the brokenness inside the drunkard; they see the root rather than the shoot. Watching this has brought about a shift in my thinking. May sometimes asks me to preach at the fellowship meeting – it is just a short talk really – and every time I agree to do something, I am the one who is blessed.

Sometimes people go to church without re-alising that they are in need. It is almost like a social outing. But people coming to Preshal know they are in need. When people recognise that they are in need, it is easier to point them to Jesus and to explain that He is able to meet all our needs, whatever they are. Almost every church, whether new or old, has its own rituals and traditions, and they have their place. But the question I ask of churches I visit is 'Is the love of Jesus being ex-pressed here?' People should see the Jesus that our lives reflect rather than the Jesus we preach, es-pecially as most people never hear Jesus preached anyway. Churches and other Christian groups, Preshal among them, are all different parts of the body of Christ. I pray that we might do that rare thing, learn to work together for His glory.

Recently May has been very conscious of the need to disciple the young Christians here, those who have been born again through Preshal. I agree that this is a necessity. She asked me if I would take a class each Sunday before the fellowship meeting. I have been doing that for a short time now. Those who come sometimes have little knowledge of the Bible, but their hearts are open and they are very keen to learn. Teaching them is like feeding hungry children.

There are similar projects to Preshal in India but there is a big difference. Most that I know about, but not all, are just fundraising organisations. There is little talk about funds in Preshal. In fact, often the talk about funds is about fundraising for other people in need. I believe that is how it should be.

When I think about the future of Preshal I feel keen for them to have a proper building. For example, there could be an adult Bible class if we only had a room quiet enough to hold it, and they really need a quiet room where people could pray. I think there will always be a place for Preshal in Linthouse. In fact, I think there is a place for Preshal in every community because every community has people in need, even if they don't recognise it.

Our daughter Elaine loves coming to the fellowship meeting and helping to lead the singing. Ann is also gifted and she uses her cooking talents to the glory of God here too. It is more blessed to give than to receive and we as a family have been greatly blessed any time we have done anything for the people who come to Preshal.

I believe that love is the strongest force that motivates and brings out the best in people. In the world we often see the use of force, but it is the force of money, muscle, politics – even religion – and its aim is to gain selfish objectives. It is really self-love. Preshal is not about self-love; it is about the love of God and about expressing His love in every way we can.

I asked Elaine how she would describe Preshal and this is what she said.

'They are loving. They are caring. They are fun. They save and raise lots of money to share it with others. They give gifts to the needy. And we have a wonderful praise and worship time on Sundays.' I think Elaine has got it just right.

Once a preacher, who had spoken at the fellowship meeting, shared with me afterwards his joy at the felt presence of Jesus. I told him that in our meetings, and in our lives outside the meetings, Jesus is Lord over everything and that we want Him to guide us in all that we do. The Lord has always graciously shown His presence in tangible ways. A church or other Christian group that feels it is self-sufficient, depending only on its physical assets, might be tempted to forget that Jesus is more important than their building and all their activities. Preshal is not like that. Of course, Sunday is not the only day on which Preshal works for Jesus. Everything that is done here, Monday to Friday as well as Sunday evening, is done for His glory.

I see Preshal as a factory. Jesus is the Chief Executive Officer, not May. She depends totally on Him. The people who come in to Preshal are precious stones. Outside of Preshal they may just be seen as rubble, but in here people look behind the dull and broken exterior of the precious stones and see what they can be in Jesus. May knows first hand what a difference Jesus can make in broken lives, and she works and watches for God's blessing. Over the last four years I have seen many lives transformed through the work of Preshal. I've seen broken stones polished and prepared to be used for the good of their families, for the good of society and for the glory of God.

12

Looking at Life's Hurts

Matt's Story

When I was a child everything was fine. Everything was normal until I was about seven when Dad took me to see my Granny Robertson (his mother) one day. It was great there. Granny gave me pieces and jam (jam sandwiches), an apple and sweeties. But when we were there I felt Dad was angry with me for something. I didn't know what. When we left, he pinned me against a fence. Shoving me hard against it, he said, 'She's not your granny. Your dad's name is …, and you're nothing!' Leaving me gasping, he stormed off and I wondered what on earth I'd done. Suddenly he spun round. 'Come here!' he roared, and I raced after him but kept at a safe distance. When we reached our house, I watched him go in and I ran away to my mates. I went home eventually to discover Dad acting as if nothing had happened! Confused, I didn't know what to say to my Ma or my brother. A couple of days later Dad got me on my own. 'Don't you dare tell your Ma or your brothers what I told you. If you do, they'll hate you as well.' From then on Dad and I lived two different lives. When we were with Ma or my brothers, he treated me just like he treated everyone else. When we were on our own – and I avoided that as often as I could – Dad tormented me and hit me hard. He told me that he hated me and I could see in his eyes that it was true.

I got really mixed up and I did things I shouldn't have done when I was a teenager. Smashing windows and things like that got rid of the feelings that boiled up inside me. Life was alright when I was with Ma, and my Grandad Burns (Ma's dad) was my hero. But Dad kept going on and on and on and on at me. Once he went into my room, called me horrible things, and threw my tapes and records and everything all over the place. I was bigger than him by then and it was my turn to pin him down. Holding him against the wall, I told him that I wasn't a child any more and that I'd really hurt him if he didn't stop what he was doing. Dad was scared.

He knew I meant what I was saying and that I was strong enough to kill him. He stopped going on at me for a while but he kept going into my room and prowling through my things. That really got to me and screwed me up inside. When I was about nineteen I asked Dad why he hated me so much. 'Because you killed my father,' he growled. 'What do you mean?' 'You killed my father,' he said again. 'The day you were baptised a Catholic, my father died.' Grandad Robertson was a Protestant. And that was meant to be my fault!

My mates and I could be sitting around drinking and taking hash and he'd come and threaten us. I don't know what he thought he could do, for we could have knocked the living daylights out of him by then. We were all stronger than he was, but he had to be the big man, the hard man. That's just how he was. I got engaged and my fiancée was pregnant. After our daughter was born, Dad succeeded in breaking us up. He called my daughter the same things he'd called me. One day I snapped and smashed three of his ribs. I'm still ashamed of that. I wasn't at the time though, because my ex-fiancée wouldn't let me see my daughter. Although I thought I was quite a hard man, I've always loved children and I missed my daughter terribly.

I worked hard Monday to Friday and then really went wild at the weekend. From Friday night on I was in the pub drinking, taking dope, dancing the night away on ecstasy, acid, speed, hash … anything I could get my hands on. I just went stupid at weekends. I was with another girl by then and she had two kids of her own. I loved them and I was over the moon when she told me she was expecting our own baby. The only thing was that seeing her pregnant ripped at my heart because I missed my daughter so much and never saw her. It still hurts all these years later. I've always wanted to be a dad to her, and she won't even speak to me.

One night I was sitting in my flat in Possil (part of Glasgow) at about 1 a.m.. The girl upstairs and her stepsister came down and invited me to a party. I went upstairs to join them. I'd only been there a few minutes when she put on a record and started to do an erotic dance in front of me. She fell backwards and I stood up to help her when something hit me on the side of the head. I didn't know it at the time, but it was a machete. I felt my head being sliced, my hand as well and, when I tried to turn round, my face was slashed. Blood poured down from my head, and it seemed black instead of red.

Staggering out of the flat and down the stairs, I still don't know how I managed to get to the police station along the road. When the desk sergeant saw the state of me, he slammed down the phone and asked what had happened as he dialled for an ambulance. I didn't really know what was happening, but I remember a policeman trying to hold bits of my head together to stop the bleeding. I blacked out, and when I came round the paramedics were there. 'Tell my kids I love them,' I heard myself saying over and over and over again. 'It's bad, mate,' one of the paramedics said. He didn't need to tell me that. I was rushed to hospital.

I don't know what happened after that until my mother and sister came in. They just saw the slashes on my face and where the doctors had joined my thumb back on again, but they didn't know I'd been done with a machete too. Then my brother came. The nurses wanted to change the dressing on the machete wounds but I wouldn't let go of my brother's hand. He had to stay through it all and he was white as the hospital sheets. 'Make sure you do a good job of him,' the policeman who had stayed with me told the nurses. 'Whatever he's done, he didn't deserve that.'

It was strange, but I was put in the same ward I'd been in as a boy when I'd broken my elbow! The next day some of the family were in, full of advice. 'Remember to say you're traumatised,' I was told. 'That way you'll get more in criminal injuries.' How could I not be traumatised with what had happened to me! And I was traumatised at the thought that the man who did it would come back and finish me off. I had to have an operation and when I first saw myself in the mirror I looked as if I'd been blown up in the trenches.

On Old Firm Day (when Rangers and Celtic Football teams play each other) I was let out of hospital as the game always fills up the ward. My brother came for me, but I was scared out of my mind as soon as I was out of the hospital. I was sure the man was waiting round every corner to finish me off. I couldn't go back to my partner for the sake of the children. She wouldn't have me anyway in case of what might happen if I was in the house. My brother took me to Ma's house and I stayed with her for about six months until I got a place of my own. Eventually my partner moved out of Glasgow to get away from me, and from the man who'd attacked me. I hated her for that. I hated her for taking the kids from me. I loved the kids.

At first I was scared to go out the door. Then I discovered that a drink gave me the courage to go out. Before long I couldn't go out unless I'd had a drink, and even then I'd only go out if I'd a mate with me. When I was in the house I needed the doors to be locked to feel safe, and even then I didn't really feel safe. Before long I started having anxiety attacks, when my whole body shook for five or ten minutes. It was horrible and frightening. I didn't tell anybody about it, but when they found out, everybody wanted to talk about it. Maybe they thought I'd get more criminal injury money because of the anxiety attacks. I just wanted them to shut up.

In 2003 I went to a counsellor and talked about what had happened to me. The counsellor asked me all kinds of questions and I ended up telling him about Dad. 'The best thing you can do is tell your family about your father,' he advised. I thought about that and then phoned Ma. She came to see me and I told her what had happened, and what Dad had said and done when I was a boy. She didn't believe a word I was saying and she was furious. When she told my brother, he went off the deep end and said I was lying too. Nobody seemed to believe me. It looked like the counsellor's advice had been all wrong.

I didn't discover what happened next right away, but Ma phoned my sister and told her. 'I know,' my sister said. 'Dad told me about five years ago.' Mum and Dad weren't together by then and Mum went round to see him. Dad admitted that he'd done and said what I'd told them. After that the family rallied round me and tried to help. Ma was upset that I'd not told her about it, but I'd known she wouldn't believe me. And the way she went on when I did tell showed me I was right.

'Come and see me at Christmas,' Dad said in 2004. But I wouldn't go. 'There are things you and I need to talk about,' he told me. I told him that after all he'd done to me I'd nothing to say to him. He'd ruined my life. He'd broken up my daughter and me. He died the next April. I saw Dad that day and I cried after he was dead. But I cried because I was so angry, not because I was sad. I wasn't. That night I went back to see my sister but she and Ma couldn't wait for me to leave. I was off drink at the time and they wanted to get to the pub. When I left them I went back home, turned my music up loud, opened a can of beer and drank it.

I was diagnosed with post traumatic stress disorder. No wonder! My Community Psychiatric nurse thought I might make friends in Preshal and took me there, stayed for an hour and a half, and then left. Although I was always scared on my own, I made friends at Preshal and started playing pool with them. On Sunday evenings there's a fellowship meeting at Preshal and May kept asking me to go to it. But I didn't want to go. Apart from anything else I was scared to go out in the dark in case I was attacked. In any case, I didn't want to know about God because I blamed Him for all that had happened to me. If He existed at all, where had He been when I needed him? At the same time, I felt as though God was trying to knock on my door and get in. So I didn't go to the Sunday meetings though I went Monday to Friday, and the more I went to Preshal the better I felt. I loved going there during the day.

I'd like to say that was the end of my drinking, but it wasn't. Last year I had a really bad time. I was drinking and someone I loved died really suddenly. I was gutted and didn't even want to go on living. Then I met Lynne and, after we moved in together, she became pregnant. I'll never forget seeing the scan photo of our baby. I was still drinking a bit, though not as much as I used to, and we had a long talk about it. I agreed to stop drinking and to stop smoking dope and to be the best dad I could be.

At the beginning of February 2008 I decided that I'd propose to Lynne on St Valentine's Day. I borrowed a ring gauge and teased her till I found out her ring size. Then I bought a ring from Argos and went to the flower shop and bought a white rose and a pink rose. They didn't have any red ones. Shaking like a leaf, I went to Preshal and went down on one knee in front of Lynne and asked her to marry me. She burst into tears, hugged me, and said yes!

I went with Lynne to the fellowship meeting and one night the man who was speaking just spoke right to me. I'd been running away from God but I couldn't run fast enough. That night I asked how I could become a Christian, and the Lord Jesus came into my heart. And do you know what happened? All the hatred that was inside me went away! I'd been full of hatred for so long that

I felt completely different. Preshal's my family now. I love the people here. I was given a Bible and started to read it. I read a bit from the New Testament and a bit from the Old Testament. It's really good! It gives me guidelines for my life. When I do something wrong God brings what the Bible says into my mind and I feel guilty. I ask God to forgive me, and He does.

A lot of my life has been spent drunk, stoned and high as a kite, but not now. I'm thirty-nine and life's precious. I've so much to look forward to, especially now that Lynne and I have a new baby son. He's called Matthew. I'm a father already but I've never been a dad before. I'm looking forward to being a Christian dad, and Lynne and I are looking forward to bringing up Matthew believing in Jesus. God will never let me down. I still make mistakes, and life still has its ups and downs, but my child won't go through what I went through with my dad. And when he hears me speaking about Jesus, I'll not be swearing, I'll be talking about the One who loved me enough to die to save me.

13

Looking at my Boy

Annette's Story

I was brought up in a Christian home with my parents and grandparents all believers in Jesus. The Christian lifestyle was all I knew. When I was seven, a younger cousin became a believer, and it was like a light switching on in my head and my heart when I realised I had to accept Jesus as my very own Saviour. No doubt I had some very strange ideas then, but the heart of the matter was in me and I grew in faith as I grew up.

In 1984 I married Jim, whom I'd known for a while through Christian youth clubs. Like me, his background is Christian. We seemed to be just made for one another, and our families and church families were pleased to see two young Christians being married. Four years later we had a miscarriage and then, after twelve long years of waiting, God gave us Jamie. Our lives were full and running over.

Jamie was a fine strong and healthy baby and I loved being a mum. My mum also loved being a gran. When Jamie was eight months old I went back to work as a director of a construction company. Mum had Jamie when I was working and things ran smoothly. About six weeks later, when Jamie was sitting feeding one day, we noticed that his eyes were droopy and the blues of his eyes looked cloudy. We were going to have a family photo taken, and on the way back we went to the hospital, but they didn't think there was anything to worry about. However, the days that followed were worrying and I was back and forth to the doctor. I imagine it was thought I was just being a fussy mum, but Jim and I were both very concerned.

In desperation, I took Jamie to Yorkhill Hospital in Glasgow a few days later and he was admitted. His face was drooping, he had stopped eating, and saliva was drooling out the sides of his mouth. The doctors were baffled and went through a whole battery of tests on our baby. By the Sunday night Jamie was very poorly. He had septicaemia and was getting worse rather than better. A few days later his airways collapsed and the crash team was called in to revive him. After two days we were faced with the awful realisation that our lovely baby boy was being kept alive by a ventilator and that we might be asked to make the decision to switch it off. Not only that, but by then the doctors were talking about Jamie having a metabolic disorder, which meant that any other children we had could have the same. We went from a happy, healthy little family to that unimaginable situation in just ten days.

Jim and I went home and the elders from our church came to pray with us. We were beginning to talk about the possibility of Jamie dying. Jim had even decided that he would carry his little coffin himself at the funeral if he did die. Then we had a phone call from the hospital. Were we anywhere near the hospital? No, we weren't. We assumed that Jamie was nearing the end and they were scared we wouldn't reach him on time, so it threw us when the consultant said that there was actually a slight improvement in his condition. I was desperate and asked God for a sign so that I'd know if Jamie was going to pull through. We loved him so much. A day or two later, when we were sitting beside his ventilator, his wee hand reached up and touched Jim's beard and started to play with it. Jim knew in his heart then that Jamie would recover.

As Jamie was a little better the doctors tried to take out the tubes but he couldn't maintain his airways and they needed to be put in again. They explained to us that the only way he would breathe on his own would be through a tracheotomy tube put into his airway through a small hole in the front of his neck. Jamie had hardly recovered from the anaesthetic after his tracheotomy surgery when he tried to pull himself up by the sides of his cot, but our poor wee boy was weaker then than the day he was born.

When Jamie was well enough he was transferred to a four-bedded ward and eventually he was discharged and we took him home, complete with his tracheotomy tube, plus all the paraphernalia for nasal gastric feeding, as he couldn't swallow anything. We lived like that until Jamie was nearly two, and in that time I resuscitated him four times when his tracheotomy tube plugged and he stopped breathing. We were trained to resuscitate him, but nothing really prepares you for doing that to your own child.

At two years old Jamie's tracheotomy was reversed and he was able to breathe on his own. With physiotherapy and speech therapy he progressed well. And that should have been such a relief for us. It was, but I reacted by going right down. I think I'd just been through so much. But Jamie went from strength to strength. He was a fast runner, and when he swam he could even hold his breath under the water! The doctors decided that he'd had brain stem encephalitis provoked by a virus and that he'd made a good recovery. They thought the problem was over, and we were very, very happy to go along with that.

I became involved with other Christian activities, including Preshal, as Jamie was doing so well. I was helping with a rough sleepers initiative and when I heard about Preshal I wondered if I might help one day a week. Jamie's condition meant I was no longer going out to work and I felt I had time to be involved. To start with I went as a volunteer one day a week. Then I joined the group visiting Shotts Prison weekly. That suited me fine as the prison isn't far from where we live. After a few months I was invited to join the Preshal staff. I was delighted and felt this was one way I could serve the Lord.

When Jamie was six, I was at a Preshal staff meeting and my phone was on silent. At the end of the meeting I discovered a message on my mobile saying that he was in our local hospital on a ventilator. There hadn't been time to take him into Glasgow for treatment. As the doctors thought that he might have suffered bleeding on his brain, Jamie was given a CAT scan, but nothing showed up on it. There was no intensive care bed in Yorkhill, so our little boy was taken by special ambulance – that was really a hospital on wheels – through to Edinburgh. The most frightening thing this time round was that there was no warning, no droopy eyes, nothing like that. In fact, the previous evening Jamie had been doing somersaults. When I thought back, he had said bye bye to me in a baby voice when I left for my meeting at Preshal. I thought he was just playing when, in fact, he was probably losing his speech. My first pay cheque from Preshal came the very day Jamie took ill. We didn't know then that I was going to have to be off work for the next year.

May came over to see us in Edinburgh, and she and a minister friend prayed with us for Jamie. Once again he was desperately ill and we didn't know if he would make it. The doctors thought it had been triggered by a virus he had caught at school. About ten boys and girls in his class had been off the previous week. In all the time since his first terrible episode until that virus, Jamie had not had a single day's illness.

As soon as a bed became available in Yorkhill our son was transferred back to Glasgow. The consultant there had seen him just four weeks previously for a routine check-up, and had been so delighted with his condition that he had taken a video of him running along the corridor. We weren't the only ones who were deeply upset, his consultant was, too. When Jamie recovered consciousness, all he could move were his eyes and he had totally lost his speech. On the following day the speech therapist started to teach us how to communicate with him responding just using his eyes. The worst case prognosis then was that that was all he might ever be able to do. He was given the same immunoglobulin treatment as he had had previously. After eight weeks in intensive care Jamie was able to give us a thumbs up sign and a one-sided smile. From then on he began to improve, despite having to have another tracheotomy, which we were told might be long term.

Jamie is now seven years old. His tracheotomy tube was removed after five months and his speech is improving. He walks with leg splints, but he gets around well. Our boy went back to school after several months off. Two weeks ago Jamie had a virus. He was taken into hospital right away and given immunoglobulin treatment. After a few days he was home again and he's now back at school. He's a real wee trooper. Thankfully not many children have Jamie's condition. In fact, it's so rare that we've not met anyone else who suffers from it.

I take Jamie to Preshal whenever I can. That's his comfort zone. Not only that, but when he's there he learns to care for other people. Everybody at Preshal cares for Jamie and he's learning to care for them.

When the new youth work was just beginning, May asked Jim if he'd like to be involved. He has a real gift in that direction and he felt the Lord was leading him into some form of Christian service, though he didn't know what it was. Now we are both involved in Preshal and the people there are part of our family life.

Because of Jamie's condition we've gone down roads we could never have imagined, but we've gone down them hand in hand with each other and hand in hand with God, and supported by our wonderful family and our Preshal (precious) friends.

When I approached May with an offer to help one day a week in Preshal, I could never have begun to imagine how much Jim and I would be helped by the people there.

14

May's last Word

Something that thrills me is that Preshal is a family that is interested in people outside of itself. It could become inward looking but that's just not happening, partly because members of my team and I go out speaking at meetings all over the country. We have associations with Kiki's work in Kilmallie, and with groups working in other places too. For example, after I spoke at a meeting in Arbroath, Jim and Tracey, who were in the group, started up an outreach called Havalah. Preshal means precious; Havalah means precious stones. They have the same vision as we do and we support them with our interest and our prayers. We also fundraise for each other.

Many of the people who come in the doors of Preshal carry huge burdens of sadness and pain and hurt. It's thrilling to watch as they find relief and healing, and some of them find new life in Jesus. Others come in to help, but they too have burdens to bear and find support in Preshal. The truth is that every single one of us needs each other. And when the needs are greatest, the support of the Preshal family is greatest too.

Ian and Jo came along and felt instantly at home. They are both clever, well-educated people brought up in Christian homes. Having come to help, they fell in love with the people and we loved them. The young couple had hoped for a family for many years but none had come along. When Jo became pregnant you would have thought the whole of Preshal was going to have a baby! We all waited expectantly for this long-awaited baby to arrive. But dear little Lucas died as he was being born. I saw the little treasure. He was so beautiful and he looked just like his dad. Preshal wrapped round Ian and Jo like a warm and comforting blanket of love and they needed that so much. Even in the sadness of their grief I never heard them grumbling against the Lord. Time has passed and God has given Ian and Jo another little son, Elliot Francis. This little baby, who could never replace Lucas, has been welcomed by loving parents into a loving home and is a member of Preshal's loving family.

Very recently another couple who should have been rejoicing were suddenly plunged into tragedy. I first met Teresa through Wellspring in Northern Ireland and she and I hit it off right away. Tom Kelly's wife Michelle and I were out walking and she had been praying for Teresa for years. She's a real example of praying without ceasing. God sometimes answers prayer right away, but this was one occasion when he delayed his answer a long time for reasons of his own. When I met Teresa, I noticed she was wearing an AA (Alcoholics Anonymous) badge.

'Are you in AA?' I asked.

She smiled. 'Are you a friend of Dr Bob and Dr Bill?' (They were the founders of AA)

'No,' I said, 'I'm a friend of Jesus, but I was an alcoholic too.'

Our conversation continued and Teresa and I got on like sisters.

Teresa had such a sad story to tell. She and her husband Patsy had lost a son and a grandson in a house fire. Their son had gone in to save his little boy, and when their bodies were found he had the wee one tucked inside his jacket to keep him safe. Not only that, but their young granddaughter had died of meningitis. My heart just went out to Teresa the more I knew about her.

Drink is a terrible scourge in Scotland at New Year and I try to arrange for the Preshal folk who've had drink problems to be safely away from temptation. One New Year we took a group of them over to Northern Ireland. Teresa and Patsy opened their home to us, and we arrived there with our shortbread and Irn Bru (Scotland's totally non-alcoholic favourite drink!) to celebrate New Year. What a great time we had. There was singing and games and lots of laughter and times of prayer too. Teresa and I had some long talks together and she even came in when we were having prayer meetings. Tom and Michelle, who had prayed for the couple for years, no doubt stepped up their prayers over that New Year holiday.

Not long afterwards Teresa and Patsy came over to Scotland, complete with Mary and Michael, Teresa's sister and brother-in-law from America, and we gave them a holiday to remember. One day we took them up to Glencoe and Michael thought that it was even more beautiful than his mountains back home! Within half an hour of arriving in the glen we had a barbecue on the table – and we had visitors. Two young off-duty policemen were more than happy to take up our offer of hamburgers and cups of tea. We always take extra food with us for anyone who wants to join us.

Teresa and Patsy were about to celebrate their golden wedding and they wanted to renew their marriage vows while they were in Scotland. My minister came to Preshal and prayed for God's blessing on them. He spoke about the golden book – the Bible, the golden gospel, and the golden way in which we walk. After the seriousness of the ceremony we had a good old Preshal party, golden wedding cake and all. Our friends were overwhelmed and were lost for words when they were given a gift by Preshal to a night in a hotel. My house was full to overflowing anyway!

When the golden couple went back home they started attending Wellspring again and, through Tom's faithful preaching of God's Word, Teresa came to faith and then Patsy did too. Patsy said that it was seeing Christianity in action that had drawn him to the Lord. In June 2008 Preshal should have been enjoying another celebration, as our friends were going to come over to Glasgow to be baptised and to make public profession of their faith in Jesus. Instead, they were mourning the death of their son.

Emmett, who was just twenty-two years old, worked delivering pizzas. He went to the aid of a lad who was involved in a fight and Emmett was murdered. One person was arrested, two handed themselves in to the police, and two sixteen-year-olds did a runner. Some boys painted 'murderer' on the houses of the lads who were thought to be involved. Patsy and Teresa's sons and grandsons went to their houses and scrubbed the paint off.

The mother of one of the accused boys went to see Teresa and Patsy. What a brave woman to do that. She was made welcome in their home and assured that she was not held responsible. Only God's grace allowed them to say that and mean it.

I went over to Northern Ireland to be with Patsy and Teresa and was blessed to see them witnessing to God's goodness in the midst of that terrible tragedy. Two days after Emmett's funeral, his baby son was born. I'd never been at a wake before. There were hundreds of people there and I'm sure there was healing in that. Since then a teenager has been charged with the murder.

We've known murders here in Govan too, and fights and knife crime are nothing unusual. I've always had a burden for teenagers because I believe that if you reach them young you can help to prevent the kind of problems that we see in Preshal; you can even help to prevent the terrible kind of violence that took Emmett's life. For about three years I prayed that God would show us the right time to start youth work in Preshal, and then last year Ebenezer Church in Motherwell raised £8,000 for a youth work pilot scheme. God seemed to be moving us on.

A few months ago young folk decided to jam the locks of Preshal with little stones, just the kind of things kids do. The following Sunday some of them were hanging about outside when we arrived for our fellowship meeting. 'We're having a meeting,' I told them. 'Come in and join us.' 'What kind of meeting?' I was asked. 'It's a Christian meeting and you can come or not, whatever you like. There's juice and crisps,' I added. A few came in and sat at the back listening for about half an hour before they left. The next day they came and apologised for jamming up the locks. That seemed to me to be another sign that the time was right to think about starting our youth work.

Alan, my son, is young and relates very well to young folk. I asked him to research the possibility of youth work and he did that, finding out what else was happening locally and contacting the police and other agencies. 'Do you want to put a notice in the local schools?' I was asked. I didn't think we should do that because the young people we wanted to reach weren't in school. They were expelled or AWOL. On the first night we opened for youth work 34 young people arrived. That was just a few weeks ago. The most we've had in one evening is 54, and 101 different youngsters have come through the door.

One lad turned up and I knew he'd been drinking. I told him he could stay that night but he'd not to come again with a drink in him. 'Is it all right if I go round the back for a joint?' he asked. Smoking cannabis is so common I don't think it occurred to him that I'd object. It breaks my heart to hear some of these kids' stories. A number are bringing themselves up! I think that young people respect authority if they know where the lines are drawn. And that seems to be working so far. Now we get 'please' and 'thank you' for the hamburgers, and litter isn't dropped around Preshal's premises. These might seem small things, but for our kids they are mountains climbed.

We had a visit from an official from the local authority. He said that he thought every community should have a centre like Preshal for its young people and that the government should be funding it. I told him that if we waited for the government, we'd wait until doomsday. The voluntary sector, especially Christian groups, are the ones who work round the clock, who will go the extra mile, the extra fifty miles. For them it's not a job, it's a ministry.

When I look back over the years since Preshal began in 2002, I thank God for lives changed out of all recognition. You've read about some of them in this book. Perhaps one day another book will be written telling of young people being diverted from petty crime, addiction, violence and eventual despair to lives of Christian service. And if that happens, it will all be down to Jesus. Preshal is only a tool in his hands; the power and the glory are His alone.